SOLDIERS FOR CHRIST

How to Be Fully Equipped for Spiritual Battle

SARAH E. LIGHTELL, MA

ISBN 979-8-89309-115-1 (Paperback)
ISBN 979-8-89309-116-8 (Digital)
Library of Congress Control Number: 2023914456

Covenant Books
11661 Hwy 707
Murrells Inlet, SC 29576
www.covenantbooks.com

Sarah Lightell expresses a heartfelt concern that the church be prepared for the hard times that loom ahead. Every saved person is a soldier for Christ. Our training is never complete. God expects us to do our duty and stand strong in these days. Truly we are in a spiritual battle. As Eph 6:12 says, "For we wrestle not against flesh and blood, but against principalities, against powers, against the rulers of the darkness of this world, against spiritual wickedness in high places." I highly recommend Sarah's book in hopes that we can all stand for Christ stronger and more courageous.

—Dr. George R. Sledd
Pastor, Jordan Baptist Church, Sanford, Florida
Author, *Blessed Assurance Jesus Is Mine:
The Eternal Hope of Christianity*

With persecution and dark influences growing daily, rough roads are ahead if you're a Christian. We must be ready for a spiritual battle. With a fantastic command of Scripture, Sarah marches us through the Word, from having a zeal for Christ to knowing the enemy and finally waiting on the Lord and rejoicing in His second coming. This book is more than a call to action; it is a roadmap for transforming average believers into battle-hardened champions of Christ. It's *The Art of War* for the Christian life. I cannot recommend it enough.

—John Fairfull
CIO, Simplicity.Online
Author, *I'm Still Writing These
Lines: Lyrics by John Fairfull*

This book is dedicated to my precious brothers and sisters in
Christ who fight the good fight for the glory of our Lord.

No man that warreth entangleth himself with the affairs of this
life; that he may please him who hath chosen him to be a soldier.

—2 Timothy 2:4

CONTENTS

PREFACE

For over two thousand years, Christians have wondered. "Is it now?" "Is this the time of Christ's coming?" "When shall the appearing of the Son of Man be?"

No man can know the day or the hour, but we are "looking for that blessed hope, and the glorious appearing of the great God and our Saviour Jesus Christ" (Titus 2:13). Christians have suffered persecution from the beginning of time, since Cain slew Abel. However, the worst is yet to come, and our Lord wants us to be ready. In Matthew 24, Jesus gives us a glimpse into these latter days:

> And Jesus answered and said unto them, Take heed that no man deceive you. For many shall come in my name, saying, I am Christ; and shall deceive many. And ye shall hear of wars and rumours of wars: see that ye be not troubled: for all these things must come to pass, but the end is not yet. For nation shall rise against nation, and kingdom against kingdom: and there shall be famines, and pestilences, and earthquakes, in divers places. All these are the beginning of sorrows. Then shall they deliver you up to be afflicted, and shall kill you: and ye shall be hated of all nations for my name's sake. And then shall many be offended, and shall betray one another, and shall hate one another. And many false prophets shall rise, and shall deceive many. And because iniquity shall abound, the love of many shall wax cold. But he that shall endure unto the

end, the same shall be saved. And this gospel of
the kingdom shall be preached in all the world
for a witness unto all nations; and then shall the
end come. (Matthew 24:4–14)

Many of these things we see in the world even now. Evil forces
are rising all around us. Christians are being demonized as people
who are not "tolerant" because they stand on their godly principles.
Now more than ever, we need Christian soldiers prepared for the
battle. It is time to get serious about our walk with God. It is time to
be *on fire for God.*

INTRODUCTION

This is a study for mature Christians who want to get serious about their walk with God as effective and confident soldiers in God's army. It's for those who desire to equip themselves for spiritual battle and who want to stand in the gap in a culture that is becoming increasingly hostile to God's Word. It is for all believers. However, only a few may be called to the front line.

Everyone serves the Lord in different ways. "Prayer warriors" are essential in the Lord's work, and the strong are to care for the weak. This study is designed for those who want to join a SWAT team of dedicated believers in the army of God. It is modeled after boot-camp training used by the military.

In the twenty-first century, there is no draft to force citizens of the United States to join. Those who sign up with a desire to serve their country are true patriots. In parallel, God seeks devoted soldiers to be in His army—men and women who are "on fire" for the Lord, standing for Christ before a wicked world. "Wherefore seeing we also are compassed about with so great a cloud of witnesses, let us lay aside every weight, and the sin which doth so easily beset us, and let us run with patience the race that is set before us" (Hebrews 12:1).

This is a call to arms that must begin at the house of God and from the pastors and elders of His church. "For if the trumpet give an uncertain sound, who shall prepare himself to the battle?" (1 Corinthians 14:8).

Chapter 1 delves into the call to arms for those who want to be on fire for God. The world is spiraling into the depths of sin. People are suffering, hurting, and dying. They need the Lord. "Therefore said he unto them, The harvest truly is great, but the labourers are few: pray ye therefore the Lord of the harvest, that he would send forth labourers into his harvest" (Luke 10:2).

A devoted Christian studies the true, unadulterated Word to see the wonderful works of God, His mighty power, and His holy plan. The Bible is fuel for the fire. Christian soldiers seek the truth. "But if from thence thou shalt seek the LORD thy God, thou shalt find him, if thou seek him with all thy heart and with all thy soul" (Deuteronomy 4:29).

Chapter 2 brings out the importance of making a commitment to God. A person enlisted in the military must affirm their allegiance to the mission. It is hard to be a good soldier if you have one foot in the world and one foot in the kingdom. "No man can serve two masters: for either he will hate the one, and love the other; or else he will hold to the one, and despise the other. Ye cannot serve God and mammon" (Matthew 6:24).

Chapter 3 lays the foundation for a true Christian soldier, putting off the deeds of the old man. There is a clear parallel here to the first steps in military boot camp. They want to break you through a true test of endurance. Similarly, the Lord breaks His people and opens their heart that the Holy Spirit may enter into the soul of man. From that point forward, there is a refining process that takes place, molding the new man into the image of God through sanctification.

Chapter 4 establishes the mission. A good soldier must be focused on the common goal. This requires perfect submission and obedience to their leader. For Christians, the captain of the army is Jesus Christ, King of kings and Lord of lords.

Chapter 5 deals with the importance of discipline and training. A good soldier must work every day to exercise body, mind, and spirit. A good Christian must strive to work out their own salvation with fear and trembling. As James says, "faith without works is dead." Faith requires action. When a soldier puts what he's learned into action, he builds strength and confidence.

Chapter 6 is critical to the "battle plan." The first step is to know the enemy.

> Be sober, be vigilant; because your adversary the devil, as a roaring lion, walketh about, seeking whom he may devour. (1 Peter 5:8)

> For we wrestle not against flesh and blood, but against principalities, against powers, against the rulers of the darkness of this world, against spiritual wickedness in high places. (Ephesians 6:12)

Chapter 7 looks at the essential component of a battle plan—faith in God. Soldiers must believe that the mission is required, the plan is the best strategy, and that their leader is fully committed to a successful mission. God's mission is the Great Commission. God's strategy is the one and only way through Jesus Christ. As the captain of the army, Christ will bring His people safely into the kingdom of God.

Chapter 8 equips the Christian soldier for battle. Ephesians 6:11 says to "put on the whole armour of God, that ye may be able to stand against the wiles of the devil." And we know that "all scripture is given by inspiration of God, and is profitable for doctrine, for reproof, for correction, for instruction in righteousness: That the man of God may be perfect, throughly furnished unto all good works" (2 Timothy 3:16–17). We can be fully equipped for the battle through the Word of God!

Chapter 9 analyzes what could be one of the most difficult military assignments—learning how to wait. A good soldier must know how to wait on the Lord. The Lord says, "Be still, and know that I am God: I will be exalted among the heathen, I will be exalted in the earth" (Psalm 46:10).

Chapter 10 celebrates the Lord's victory in all things. "Thine, O Lord, is the greatness, and the power, and the glory, and the victory, and the majesty: for all that is in the heaven and in the earth is thine; thine is the kingdom, O Lord, and thou art exalted as head above all" (1 Chronicles 29:11).

As Psalm 98:1 says, "O sing unto the Lord a new song; for he hath done marvellous things: his right hand, and his holy arm, hath gotten him the victory." And we know that "for whatsoever is born of God overcometh the world: and this is the victory that overcometh the world, even our faith" (1 John 5:4). "But thanks be to God, which giveth us the victory through our Lord Jesus Christ" (1 Corinthians 15:57).

1

BE ON FIRE FOR GOD
PRAY FOR GOD'S LEADERSHIP
AND ANOINTING POWER

Summary

Chapter 1 delves into the call to arms for those who want to be on fire for God. The world is spiraling into the depths of sin. People are struggling, suffering, and dying. They need the Lord. "Therefore said he unto them, The harvest truly is great, but the labourers are few: pray ye therefore the Lord of the harvest, that he would send forth labourers into his harvest" (Luke 10:2).

So the first question is, do you want to be on fire for God? A devoted Christian studies the true, unadulterated Word to see the wonderful works of God, His mighty power, and His holy plan. The Bible is fuel for the fire. Christian soldiers seek the truth—the one and only truth, which is the Word. As Jesus says, "I am the way, the truth, and the life: no man cometh unto the Father, but by me" (John 14:6).

> In the beginning was the Word, and the
> Word was with God, and the Word was God.
> (John 1:1)

> And the Word was made flesh, and dwelt
> among us, (and we beheld his glory, the glory as
> of the only begotten of the Father,) full of grace
> and truth. (John 1: 14)

If you want to be on fire for God, you want to know the truth! "But if from thence thou shalt seek the Lord thy God, thou shalt find him, if thou seek him with all thy heart and with all thy soul" (Deuteronomy 4:29).

Are you willing to do what it takes to be on fire for God? If not, why not? What it takes is devotion—a sincere love for God and His people, a sincere desire to share the gospel. Those who seek to be a true disciple can say, "Lord, touch my lips with your burning coal, as Isaiah, and feed me with your scroll, as Jeremiah."

> Let the words of my mouth, and the med-
> itation of my heart, be acceptable in thy sight,
> O Lord, my strength, and my redeemer. (Psalm
> 19:14)

> For He that is mighty hath done to me great
> things; and holy is his name. (Luke 1:49)

Pray to hear these precious words from our Savior, "Well done, good and faithful servant; thou hast been faithful over a few things, I will make thee ruler over many things: enter thou into the joy of thy Lord" (Matthew 25:23). You do not want your earthly desires to choke out your spiritual growth.

The question is, how can a believer be on fire for God? What revives a person to the zeal of their first encounter with Christ? How does one keep any relationship alive—and not just alive but thriving?

The answer is investment—spending time studying the Bible, praying, fellowship, and in outreach. "But this I say, He which soweth sparingly shall reap also sparingly; and he which soweth bountifully shall reap also bountifully" (2 Corinthians 9:6). The Christian soldier sows the depths of the soul of man with great compassion. Each relationship is built on the love of Christ. "They that sow in tears shall reap in joy" (Psalm 126:5). And there is no greater joy than seeing the Lord save a soul through Christ in you. That is the joy that truly sets the heart on fire for the Lord.

The key words are "through Christ in you." Any work for the Lord requires the anointing power of the Holy Spirit—the fire of God. "The things which are impossible with men are possible with God" (Luke 18:27). A Christian soldier starts and ends his day on his knees, praying without ceasing. For example, before I begin writing, I pray for the mind of Christ—that it would be His words and not mine that make their way to the page. It is amazing what happens when we are filled with His Holy Spirit!

Your desire must be grounded in faith to blossom and thrive. "Therefore I say unto you, What things soever ye desire, when ye pray, believe that ye receive them, and ye shall have them" (Mark 11:24). That kind of desire blossoms into joy, as the scripture says, "Delight thyself also in the LORD; and he shall give thee the desires of thine heart" (Psalm 37:4). The more we joy in the Lord, the more His light shines through us. "Rejoice in the Lord alway: and again I say, Rejoice" (Philippians 4:4).

What is the desire of your heart? A spiritual zeal can grow within us as we learn from the mighty men who were on fire for God in the Bible. From the beginning, God has called out His warriors for His holy purpose. Noah was called by God to build an ark in the midst of a dry and wicked land. The Lord chose him, and "Noah found grace in the eyes of the LORD," as we see in Genesis 6.

> And God saw that the wickedness of man
> was great in the earth, and that every imagina-
> tion of the thoughts of his heart was only evil
> continually. And it repented the LORD that he
> had made man on the earth, and it grieved him
> at his heart. And the LORD said, I will destroy
> man whom I have created from the face of the
> earth; both man, and beast, and the creeping
> thing, and the fowls of the air; for it repenteth me

> that I have made them. But Noah found grace
> in the eyes of the LORD. These are the genera-
> tions of Noah: Noah was a just man and perfect
> in his generations, and Noah walked with God.
> (Genesis 6:5–9)

In these verses, we see the fire in Noah's heart. His saving knowledge of the Lord God Almighty gave him the desire to strive to be just and perfect. Just like Adam, Noah walked with God. That personal relationship is where the fire begins. Noah's love of God, his submission, and his obedience ignited that fire through the power of the Holy Spirit. The first commandment is the most important one. *How much do we love the Lord?* Another question might be, *how is your walk with the Lord?*

The Lord saved Noah and called him to be a soldier.

> And God said unto Noah, The end of all
> flesh is come before me; for the earth is filled
> with violence through them; and, behold, I will
> destroy them with the earth. Make thee an ark of
> gopher wood; rooms shalt thou make in the ark,
> and shalt pitch it within and without with pitch.
> (Genesis 6:13–14)

> Thus did Noah; according to all that God
> commanded him, so did he. (Genesis 6:22)

We need to be "sold out" for the Lord, just like Noah, ready to do His will without hesitation. This is easier said than done in the face of tremendous fear. Imagine how Noah must have felt when he learned that the whole world would be destroyed? That kind of fear can be overwhelming. However, it is during such times that we need to trust in our Lord.

As Isaiah 8:13–14 says,

> Sanctify the LORD of hosts himself; and let him be your fear, and let him be your dread. And he shall be for a sanctuary; but for a stone of stumbling and for a rock of offence to both the houses of Israel, for a gin and for a snare to the inhabitants of Jerusalem.

The question is, why is it so hard to be "sold out" for the Lord? Fear can be one of our greatest roadblocks. As 1 John 4:18–19 says, "There is no fear in love; but perfect love casteth out fear: because fear hath torment. He that feareth is not made perfect in love."

Noah faced his fear, and he also faced great persecution. He preached as he built the ark, possibly for 120 years, knowing the judgment that was to come. For we know that the Lord "spared not the old world, but saved Noah the eighth person, a preacher of righteousness, bringing in the flood upon the world of the ungodly" (2 Peter 2:5). He was in the midst of the fire of God, but he remained faithful. As Hebrews 11:7 says, "By faith Noah, being warned of God of things not seen as yet, moved with fear, prepared an ark to the saving of his house; by the which he condemned the world, and became heir of the righteousness which is by faith."

Do we, being warned of God of things not seen as yet, move with fear to become Christian soldiers? Isaiah 41:10 says, "Fear thou not; for I am with thee: be not dismayed; for I am thy God: I will strengthen thee; yea, I will help thee; yea, I will uphold thee with the right hand of my righteousness."

Noah remained hopeful as the ark moved through the waters of death and destruction. The Lord shut the door on the ungodly but promised a new life for him and his family. We know that sin, once again, raised its ugly head in the new land. How quickly mankind can succumb to the darkness and lose the light of the fire. It is a constant battle. The Lord says to beware. "Ye therefore, beloved, seeing ye know these things before, beware lest ye also, being led away with the error of the wicked, fall from your own stedfastness" (2 Peter 3:17).

Why is it so easy to fall from your own steadfastness? One of the most important lessons we learn from Noah is that he walked with God even when it seemed impossible. That reminds us of what Jesus said in Mark 9:23, "If thou canst believe, all things are possible to him that believeth," and in Luke 18:27, when He said, "The things which are impossible with men are possible with God." We need to be ready "in season and out of season." The Lord calls those who are ready. When He calls, our faith must override our fear, and then the secret is perseverance. It is not easy, but "I can do all things through Christ which strengthens me" (Philippians 4:13).

What might it mean to be ready out of season? Second Timothy 4 tells us that it is sharing the Word of God "when they will not endure sound doctrine." It will require patience and perseverance amidst great persecution.

> I charge thee therefore before God, and the Lord Jesus Christ, who shall judge the quick and the dead at his appearing and his kingdom; Preach the word; be instant in season, out of season; reprove, rebuke, exhort with all longsuffering and doctrine. For the time will come when they will not endure sound doctrine; but after their own lusts shall they heap to themselves teachers, having itching ears; And they shall turn away their ears from the truth, and shall be turned unto fables. But watch thou in all things, endure afflictions, do the work of an evangelist, make full proof of thy ministry. (2 Timothy 4:1–5)

Abraham, like Noah, was called by God for a mission that would impact the whole world. His ministry began with similar words—"walk before me, and be thou perfect." His encounter with the Lord must have been overwhelming because "Abram fell on his face," as we see in Genesis 17.

> And when Abram was ninety years old and
> nine, the Lord appeared to Abram, and said unto
> him, I am the Almighty God; walk before me,
> and be thou perfect. And I will make my cov-
> enant between me and thee, and will multiply
> thee exceedingly. And Abram fell on his face: and
> God talked with him, saying, As for me, behold,
> my covenant is with thee, and thou shalt be a
> father of many nations. (Genesis 17:1–4)

God is calling today for those who will step out in faith, remembering that "His covenant is with thee." Those who respond to God's call will have the anointing of the Holy Spirit to obey His commands, and they will have the wisdom of God to understand. We, like Abraham in Sodom and Gomorrah, stand in the midst of a crooked and perverse nation, asking the same question, "Wilt thou also destroy the righteous with the wicked?" (Genesis 18:23). The Word of God is clear that the wheat must grow up with the tares, and in these latter days, the tares are very strong.

Does God destroy the righteous with the wicked? The Lord saved Noah and his family and destroyed all of the *ungodly* left behind. The Lord saved Lot and his family and destroyed all who remained in Sodom and Gomorrah. And in Ezekiel 14, we see the Lord nam-ing three men who would escape the judgement—Noah, Daniel, and Job. These were truly men on fire for the Lord!

> The word of the LORD came again to me,
> saying, Son of man, when the land sinneth
> against me by trespassing grievously, then will I
> stretch out mine hand upon it, and will break
> the staff of the bread thereof, and will send fam-
> ine upon it, and will cut off man and beast from
> it: Though these three men, Noah, Daniel, and

Job, were in it, they should deliver but their own
souls by their righteousness, saith the Lord God.
(Ezekiel 14:12–14)

Why might the Lord have named these three men in particular?

- "Noah was a just man and perfect in his generations, and Noah walked with God" (Genesis 6:9).
- "Daniel purposed in his heart" to obey God rather than man (Daniel 1:8).
- "And the LORD said unto Satan, Hast thou considered my servant Job, that there is none like him in the earth, a perfect and an upright man, one that feareth God, and escheweth evil?" (Job 1:8).

Jacob's son Joseph is another mighty man of God. He must have been horrified when his brothers left him in a pit to die and the Egyptians took him into bondage. He did not, however, remain in a stupor but committed to doing his best in every situation.

As the Bible says, "And whatsoever ye do, do it heartily, as to the Lord, and not unto men" (Colossians 3:23). Joseph's masters, and even Pharaoh, rewarded him for his loyalty. His brothers meant it for evil, but God meant it for good. And because of Joseph's faithfulness, God used him to preserve the life of his family—the twelve tribes of Israel. We need to follow in the footsteps of Joseph, not dwelling in self-pity but remaining faithful even when surrounded by the wicked, for this is the soldier's higher calling.

What do we often say? "Woe is me," and "Why did this happen to me?" As such, why is it so hard to overcome our emotions? The Lord drew Moses out of the water and into the house of Pharaoh in preparation for his calling. We need not be discouraged when it seems like everything is going against us. The Lord works in mysterious ways! Exodus 3 gives us a little insight.

Now Moses kept the flock of Jethro his
father in law, the priest of Midian: and he led the

flock to the backside of the desert, and came to the mountain of God, even to Horeb. And the angel of the LORD appeared unto him in a flame of fire out of the midst of a bush: and he looked, and, behold, the bush burned with fire, and the bush was not consumed. And Moses said, I will now turn aside, and see this great sight, why the bush is not burnt. And when the LORD saw that he turned aside to see, God called unto him out of the midst of the bush, and said, Moses, Moses. And he said, Here am I. And he said, Draw not nigh hither: put off thy shoes from off thy feet, for the place whereon thou standest is holy ground. (Exodus 3:1–5)

Moreover, he said, I am the God of thy father, the God of Abraham, the God of Isaac, and the God of Jacob. And Moses hid his face; for he was afraid to look upon God. And the LORD said, I have surely seen the affliction of my people which are in Egypt, and have heard their cry by reason of their taskmasters; for I know their sorrows; And I am come down to deliver them out of the hand of the Egyptians, and to bring them up out of that land unto a good land and a large, unto a land flowing with milk and honey; unto the place of the Canaanites, and the Hittites, and the Amorites, and the Perizzites, and the Hivites, and the Jebusites. Now therefore, behold, the cry of the children of Israel is come unto me: and I have also seen the oppression wherewith the Egyptians oppress them. Come now therefore, and I will send thee unto Pharaoh, that thou mayest bring forth my people the children of Israel out of Egypt. (Exodus 3:6–10)

Moses had learned the ways of the Egyptians and witnessed the sufferings of God's chosen people. Just like Paul on the road to Damascus, Moses had a life-changing encounter with Almighty God.

Moses was saved, called, and obedient, "choosing rather to suffer affliction with the people of God, than to enjoy the pleasures of sin for a season" (Hebrews 11:25). That is the challenge for the Christian soldier. We need the faith and courage to suffer for Christ, as 1 Peter 4:16 says, "Yet if any man suffer as a Christian, let him not be ashamed; but let him glorify God on this behalf." We can endure great suffering through the power of the Holy Spirit when we know it is the will of God.

> Wherefore let them that suffer according to
> the will of God commit the keeping of their souls
> to him in well doing, as unto a faithful Creator.
> (1 Peter 4:19)

> For God hath not given us the spirit of fear;
> but of power, and of love, and of a sound mind.
> (2 Timothy 1:7)

Are we willing to stand with the Christian soldiers and suffer affliction for the cause of Christ? This is where our faith is really tested. Another lesson we can learn from Moses is to trust in the power of God rather than be intimidated by the power of a world leader—in this case, Pharaoh.

In faith, Moses took his rod and stood before Pharaoh, as God instructed. He must have been very encouraged when his rod turned into a serpent and very discouraged when Pharaoh's sorcerers did the same. Moses stood firm in spite of his fears and performed all of the miracles through the anointing power of the Holy Spirit. This is the fire of God that we can have if we have a sincere desire to be His warrior. It will be scary. However, we can depend on God to walk with us through the fire. For we know from the book of Joel that there will be another time of signs and wonders.

> And it shall come to pass afterward, that I will pour out my spirit upon all flesh; and your sons and your daughters shall prophesy, your old men shall dream dreams, your young men shall see visions: And also upon the servants and upon the handmaids in those days will I pour out my spirit. (Joel 2:28–29)

Our world is crumbling around us—earthquakes, wars, evil empires, wickedness in high places, worldwide epidemics, food shortages, the threat of a financial collapse, and AI being used as a weapon against us—however, we know that "no weapon that is formed against thee shall prosper; and every tongue that shall rise against thee in judgment thou shalt condemn. This is the heritage of the servants of the Lord, and their righteousness is of me, saith the LORD" (Isaiah 54:17).

The Lord is preparing His called-out people for the final battle so that we are not caught off guard. In Revelation 2:10, we read, "Fear none of those things which thou shalt suffer: behold, the devil shall cast some of you into prison, that ye may be tried; and ye shall have tribulation ten days: be thou faithful unto death, and I will give thee a crown of life."

Joshua and Caleb were the only two brave witnesses to give a good report on the Promised Land. The last two witnesses, called by God, also will stand fast in front of the whole world, declaring the truth, as seen in Revelation:

> And there was given me a reed like unto a rod: and the angel stood, saying, Rise, and measure the temple of God, and the altar, and them that worship therein. But the court which is without the temple leave out, and measure it not; for it is given unto the Gentiles: and the holy city shall

they tread under foot forty and two months. And I will give power unto my two witnesses, and they shall prophesy a thousand two hundred and three-score days, clothed in sackcloth. These are the two olive trees, and the two candlesticks standing before the God of the earth. And if any man will hurt them, fire proceedeth out of their mouth, and devoureth their enemies: and if any man will hurt them, he must in this manner be killed. These have power to shut heaven, that it rain not in the days of their prophecy: and have power over waters to turn them to blood, and to smite the earth with all plagues, as often as they will. And when they shall have finished their testimony, the beast that ascendeth out of the bottomless pit shall make war against them, and shall overcome them, and kill them. (Revelation 11:1–7)

And their dead bodies shall lie in the street of the great city, which spiritually is called Sodom and Egypt, where also our Lord was crucified. And they of the people and kindreds and tongues and nations shall see their dead bodies three days and an half, and shall not suffer their dead bodies to be put in graves. And they that dwell upon the earth shall rejoice over them, and make merry, and shall send gifts one to another; because these two prophets tormented them that dwelt on the earth. And after three days and an half the Spirit of life from God entered into them, and they stood upon their feet; and great fear fell upon them which saw them. And they heard a great voice from heaven saying unto them, Come up hither. And they ascended up to heaven in a cloud; and their enemies beheld them. And the same hour was there a great earthquake, and the

> tenth part of the city fell, and in the earthquake
> were slain of men seven thousand: and the rem-
> nant were affrighted, and gave glory to the God
> of heaven. (Revelation 11:8–13)

The end times will be scary and also exciting as we see the strong hand of God moving. Jesus performed many miracles during His time on earth. And of course, there was the great anointing of the Holy Spirit on the day of Pentecost. The disciples also experienced the ability to perform miracles. However, Christ cautioned them against the temptation of pride.

It is very exciting to be on fire for the Lord. However, that kind of zeal must be tempered with a humble heart. "Let your speech be always with grace, seasoned with salt, that ye may know how ye ought to answer every man" (Colossians 4:6). And we do need to be ready at any moment to be used by God. For as the darkness comes over the earth, there will be some who will be seeking the Lord for hope. As 1 Peter 3:15 says, "But sanctify the Lord God in your hearts: and be ready always to give an answer to every man that asketh you a reason of the hope that is in you with meekness and fear."

God requires a humble heart. "And whosoever shall exalt himself shall be abased; and he that shall humble himself shall be exalted" (Matthew 23:12). For "what doth the Lord require of thee, but to do justly, and to love mercy, and to walk humbly with thy God?" (Micah 6:8). And Psalm 10:17 says it so well: "Lord, thou hast heard the desire of the humble: thou wilt prepare their heart, thou wilt cause thine ear to hear."

Christians need to be on fire for the Lord now more than ever. This time we are living in could very well be the "beginning of sorrows," a time of signs and wonders once again. The purpose, most certainly, will be to draw the last saints into the kingdom of God. It will be exciting to see the Lord work through His soldiers, but they must remember the Lord's words in Luke:

> And the seventy returned again with joy,
> saying, Lord, even the devils are subject unto

us through thy name. And he said unto them, I beheld Satan as lightning fall from heaven. Behold, I give unto you power to tread on serpents and scorpions, and over all the power of the enemy: and nothing shall by any means hurt you. Notwithstanding in this rejoice not, that the spirits are subject unto you; but rather rejoice, because your names are written in heaven. (Luke 10:17–20)

The Lord revealed Himself to Moses in the burning bush, and the bush was not consumed. Three Jewish men were in the fiery furnace, and they were not consumed. "It is of the LORD's mercies that we are not consumed, because his compassions fail not" (Lamentations 3:22). The believer wants to be on fire for God, not in the fire of God. "For our God is a consuming fire" (Hebrews 12:29). Perfect submission and humble obedience are required.

Jeremiah 23:29 reminds us that it is the Lord's fire, not our own. "Is not my word like as a fire? saith the LORD; and like a hammer that breaketh the rock in pieces?" A good soldier must always honor the King of kings and Lord of lords and obey His commandments. This is how the believer overcomes the world and wins the victory! As seen in 1 John 5, if we really love God, we will keep His commandments. This obedience will keep the fire burning.

Whosoever believeth that Jesus is the Christ is born of God: and every one that loveth him that begat loveth him also that is begotten of him. By this we know that we love the children of God, when we love God, and keep his commandments. For this is the love of God, that we keep his commandments: and his commandments are not grievous. For whatsoever is born of God overcometh the world: and this is the victory that overcometh the world, even our faith. (1 John 5:1–4)

The Lord wants His children to know His will revealed through His Word and to make known the mystery. "And without controversy great is the mystery of godliness: God was manifest in the flesh, justified in the Spirit, seen of angels, preached unto the Gentiles, believed on in the world, received up into glory" (1 Timothy 3:16). Simply stated, Jesus is God. "In the beginning was the Word, and the Word was with God, and the Word was God" (John 1:1). He wants His children to be filled with the knowledge of His will and to "make known the mystery!"

> For this cause we also, since the day we heard it, do not cease to pray for you, and to *desire* that ye might be *filled with the knowledge of his will* in all wisdom and spiritual understanding; That ye might walk worthy of the Lord unto all pleasing, being fruitful in every good work, and *increasing in the knowledge of God*; Strengthened with all might, according to his glorious power, unto all patience and longsuffering with joyfulness. (Colossians 1:9–11, emphasis mine)

When we are filled with the knowledge of His will, we can know the *mystery*. The Lord wants us to know. "And he said unto them, Unto you it is given to know the mystery of the kingdom of God: but unto them that are without, all these things are done in parables" (Mark 4:11). And how can we know the mystery? "Whereby, when ye read, ye may understand my knowledge in the mystery of Christ" (Ephesians 3:4).

- *We need to plug into the source of all power—the mind of Christ.* "For who hath known the mind of the Lord, that he may instruct him? But we have the mind of Christ" (1 Corinthians 2:16). We need to "get in the game." This battle is real. It's a matter of life and death. We need to be serious about our walk with God.

- *We must be accountable*, as James 5:16 says, "Confess your faults one to another, and pray one for another, that ye may be healed. The effectual fervent prayer of a righteous man availeth much."
- *We must fast and pray*, as Matthew 6:17 says, "But thou, when thou fastest, anoint thine head, and wash thy face."
- *We must seek the Lord "with our whole heart,"* as Jeremiah 33:3 says, "Call unto me, and I will answer thee, and shew thee great and mighty things, which thou knowest not."
- *We must reverence the Lord*, as Proverbs 9:10 says, "The fear of the LORD is the beginning of wisdom: and the knowledge of the holy is understanding."
- *We must abide in the Lord*, as John 15:5 says, "I am the vine, ye are the branches: He that abideth in me, and I in him, the same bringeth forth much fruit: for without me ye can do nothing."

These are the kinds of things the Christian soldier does "that he may please him who hath chosen him to be a soldier" (2 Timothy 2:4b). We do not please Him when we grieve the Holy Spirit.

The Lord's Word says not to grieve the Holy Spirit, so how can a Christian be on fire for Christ if he is dismayed, anxious, fearful, or depressed? These things hinder the work of the Holy Spirit. As Ecclesiastes 3:4 says, "There is a time to mourn," but it is important not to get entangled in the bondage of emotions. A Christian soldier must learn to let go of the things that pull the spirit of man down. The Lord is clear in His Word that we are not to be dismayed.

> Have not I commanded thee? Be strong and of a good courage; be not afraid, neither be thou dismayed: for the LORD thy God is with thee whithersoever thou goest. (Joshua 1:9)

> And Joshua said unto them, Fear not, nor be dismayed, be strong and of good courage:

for thus shall the LORD do to all your enemies against whom ye fight. (Joshua 10:25)

And the LORD, he it is that doth go before thee; he will be with thee, he will not fail thee, neither forsake thee: fear not, neither be dismayed. (Deuteronomy 31:8)

Fear thou not; for I am with thee: be not dismayed; for I am thy God: I will strengthen thee; yea, I will help thee; yea, I will uphold thee with the right hand of my righteousness. (Isaiah 41:10)

Thou therefore gird up thy loins, and arise, and speak unto them all that I command thee: be not dismayed at their faces, lest I confound thee before them. (Jeremiah 1:17)

Thus saith the LORD, Learn not the way of the heathen, and be not dismayed at the signs of heaven; for the heathen are dismayed at them. (Jeremiah 10:2)

Then shalt thou prosper, if thou takest heed to fulfil the statutes and judgments which the LORD charged Moses with concerning Israel: be strong, and of good courage; dread not, nor be dismayed. (1 Chronicles 22:13)

When we get our eye off the Lord and onto the things of this world, it won't be long before we are dismayed. Just as Peter looked into the eyes of Jesus and walked on the water but then quickly sank as he looked down, we make conscious and subconscious choices that determine our focus. For example, background noise—the noise of the world—is just that until we choose to pay attention to a sound and listen for details of what is being said.

The spiritual realm is much the same way. We can focus on the outward appearance of a person or look into their eyes and begin to understand their thoughts and feelings. So one of the secrets of being on fire for God is focusing on Him and the souls of His people. "Set your affection on things above, not on things on the earth" (Colossians 3:2).

2

MAKE A COMMITMENT TO GOD
HONOR THE COVENANT

Summary

This chapter brings out the importance of making a commitment to God. A person enlisted in the military must affirm their allegiance to the mission. It is hard to be a good soldier if you have one foot in the world and one foot in the kingdom. "No man can serve two masters: for either he will hate the one, and love the other; or else he will hold to the one, and despise the other. Ye cannot serve God and mammon" (Matthew 6:24). The Lord established His commitment to His people, first under the Law and second, under grace. He always keeps His part of the commitment.

The question is, do you keep your commitment to God? In the Old Testament, the Lord made a covenant. This is an agreement between two—the Lord and His people. God's holy plan is all about His relationship with His people for His pleasure and for His glory. The Word of God is His covenant, revealed in the book of the covenant and the blood of the covenant, as seen in Exodus 24.

> And he took the *book of the covenant*, and
> read in the audience of the people: and they said,
> All that the LORD hath said will we do, and be
> obedient. And Moses took the blood, and sprin-

19

kled it on the people, and said, Behold the *blood
of the covenant*, which the LORD hath made with
you concerning all these words. (Exodus 24:7–8)

We know that the book of the covenant is His Word, and the blood of the covenant is His sacrifice. Our first response should be to fall on our knees and thank Him for His "unspeakable gift!" Moses brought the Word down from the mount that burned with fire in two stone tables (Deuteronomy 9:15). Isn't it interesting to see how the stones were broken because the people had broken their commitment to God and the second set was secured in the ark of the covenant? We see this in Deuteronomy 10:8, "At that time the LORD separated the tribe of Levi, to bear *the ark of the covenant* of the LORD, to stand before the LORD to minister unto him, and to bless in his name, unto this day."

The covenant embodies the promises of God to His people: "Know therefore that the Lord thy God, he is God, the faithful God, which keepeth covenant and mercy with them that love him and keep his commandments to a thousand generations" (Deuteronomy 7:9). God's people could not fulfill their part of the covenant, "for all have sinned and come short of the glory of God" (Romans 3:23). Therefore, He provided a "new and living way, which he hath consecrated for us, through the *veil*, that is to say, *his flesh*" (Hebrews 10:20). "For if that first covenant had been faultless, then should no place have been sought for the second" (Hebrews 8:7).

For if that first covenant had been faultless,
then should no place have been sought for the
second. For finding fault with them, he saith,
Behold, the days come, saith the Lord, when I
will make a new covenant with the house of Israel
and with the house of Judah: Not according to
the covenant that I made with their fathers in the
day when I took them by the hand to lead them
out of the land of Egypt; because they continued
not in my covenant, and I regarded them not,

> saith the Lord. *For this is the covenant that I will make with the house of Israel after those days, saith the Lord; I will put my laws into their mind, and write them in their hearts: and I will be to them a God, and they shall be to me a people.* (Hebrews 8:7–10)

The new covenant, like the old, is between two—the Lord and His people. It is important to realize our part in this covenant—our commitment to God. This should not be taken lightly. We must remember that the covenant is signed with the blood of our Lord and Savior, Jesus Christ. As Hebrews 12:24 says, "And to Jesus the mediator of the new covenant, and to the blood of sprinkling, that speaketh better things than that of Abel." Romans 11:27 states it plainly: "For this is my covenant unto them, when I shall take away their sins."

Ecclesiastes 12:13 helps us understand that our commitment to God is not an option. What does it say? "Let us hear the conclusion of the whole matter: Fear God, and keep his commandments: for this is the *whole duty of man*." God is faithful even if we are not. "If we believe not, yet he abideth faithful: he cannot deny himself" (2 Timothy 2:13). Jesus Christ is the Word (of His covenant), and He changes not. As Hebrews 13:8 says, "Jesus Christ the same yesterday, and to day, and for ever." *His covenant is immutable.* He confirms this in Matthew 5:17, "Think not that I am come to destroy the law, or the prophets: I am not come to destroy, but to fulfil." The Lord also confirms His covenant by an oath:

> Wherein God, willing more abundantly to shew unto the heirs of promise the immutability of his counsel, confirmed it by an oath: That by two immutable things, in which it was impossible for God to lie, we might have a strong consolation, who have fled for refuge to lay hold upon the hope set before us: Which hope we have as an anchor of the soul, both sure and stedfast, and

which entereth into that within the veil; Whither
the forerunner is for us entered, even Jesus,
made an high priest for ever after the order of
Melchisedec. (Hebrews 6:17–20)

What are two immutable things? The Lord never changes, and
His Word never changes.

> For I am the LORD, I change not. (Malachi
> 3:6)

> For ever, O LORD, thy word is settled in
> heaven. (Psalm 119:89)

> For all flesh is as grass, and all the glory of
> man as the flower of grass. The grass withereth,
> and the flower thereof falleth away: But the word
> of the Lord endureth for ever. And this is the
> word which by the gospel is preached unto you.
> (1 Peter 1:24–25)

In the Old Testament, circumcision was the token of the covenant (Genesis 17:11), symbolic of the better covenant to come, "putting off the body of the sins of the flesh by the circumcision of Christ"
(Colossians 2:11). In the New Testament, it is the *operation of God.*

> Beware lest any man spoil you through
> philosophy and vain deceit, after the tradition of
> men, after the rudiments of the world, and not
> after Christ. *For in him dwelleth all the fulness of*
> *the Godhead bodily.* And ye are complete in him,
> which is the head of all principality and power:
> *In whom also ye are circumcised with the circum-*
> *cision made without hands, in putting off the body*
> *of the sins of the flesh by the circumcision of Christ:*
> Buried with him in baptism, wherein also ye are

risen with him through the faith of the *operation of God*, who hath raised him from the dead. (Colossians 2:8–12)

The Lord performs His operation on His people. "For we are his workmanship, created in Christ Jesus unto good works, which God hath before ordained that we should walk in them" (Ephesians 2:10). One of the first steps in being a good soldier for Christ is to be devoted to Him, "the God of peace, that brought again from the dead our Lord Jesus, that great shepherd of the sheep, through the blood of the everlasting covenant" (Hebrews 13:20). This is our personal responsibility. We must trust in the Lord to empower us for His service and be committed to do His will.

Are we willing to say with Isaiah, "I heard the voice of the Lord, saying, Whom shall I send, and who will go for us? Then said I, Here am I; send me" (Isaiah 6:8)? This commitment to the Lord is very serious, much like a vow, a measure of our devotion. Numbers 30:2 says, "If a man vow a vow unto the LORD, or swear an oath to bind his soul with a bond; he shall not break his word, he shall do according to all that proceedeth out of his mouth."

These words are seen in Deuteronomy 23:21–22 as well: "When thou shalt vow a vow unto the LORD thy God, thou shalt not slack to pay it: for the LORD thy God will surely require it of thee; and it would be sin in thee. But if thou shalt forbear to vow, it shall be no sin in thee."

One of the worst things we can do is vow and not pay, as seen in Ecclesiastes 5:4–5,

> When thou vowest a vow unto God, defer not to pay it; for he hath no pleasure in fools: pay that which thou hast vowed. Better is it that thou shouldest not vow, than that thou shouldest vow and not pay.

Psalm 76:11 also tells us to "vow, and pay unto the Lord your God: let all that be round about him bring presents unto him that ought to be feared."

Are you willing to make a vow to the Lord? Daniel was willing. As we read in the first chapter of the book of Daniel when he "purposed in his heart" to stay true to his godly principles and serve the Lord even under the threats of Nebuchadnezzar, king of Babylon.

> In the third year of the reign of Jehoiakim king of Judah came Nebuchadnezzar king of Babylon unto Jerusalem, and besieged it. And the Lord gave Jehoiakim king of Judah into his hand, with part of the vessels of the house of God: which he carried into the land of Shinar to the house of his god; and he brought the vessels into the treasure house of his god. And the king spake unto Ashpenaz the master of his eunuchs, that he should bring certain of the children of Israel, and of the king's seed, and of the princes; Children in whom was no blemish, but *well favoured*, and *skilful in all wisdom*, and *cunning in knowledge*, and *understanding science*, and such as had *ability in them to stand in the king's palace*, and *whom they might teach* the learning and the tongue of the Chaldeans. And the king appointed them a daily provision of the king's meat, and of the wine which he drank: so nourishing them three years, that at the end thereof they might stand before the king. Now among these were of the children of Judah, Daniel, Hananiah, Mishael, and Azariah: Unto whom the prince of the eunuchs gave names: for he gave unto Daniel the name of Belteshazzar; and to Hananiah, of Shadrach; and to Mishael, of Meshach; and to Azariah, of Abednego. *But Daniel purposed in his heart* that he would not defile himself with

the portion of the king's meat, nor with the wine which he drank: therefore he requested of the prince of the eunuchs that he might not defile himself. (Daniel 8:1–8)

The Lord called on Daniel and his friends because He knew their heart. Verse 4 says that they were "well favoured, and skilful in all wisdom, and cunning in knowledge, and understanding science, and such as had ability in them to stand in the king's palace, and whom they might teach the learning and the tongue of the Chaldeans." In application to our time in history, this might be interpreted as one with a good reputation, dependent on wisdom from above to guide their decisions, filled with the knowledge of God's Word, anxious to learn, and easily taught. Most importantly, Daniel loved the Lord and wanted to please Him. That is the heart of a soldier for Christ!

Of course, we know that Shadrach, Meshach, and Abednego showed tremendous courage as well, choosing not to bow to the king's idol. Their faith was in the Lord, whether they burned in the furnace or not.

> Shadrach, Meshach, and Abednego, answered and said to the king, O Nebuchadnezzar, we are not careful to answer thee in this matter. If it be so, our God whom we serve is able to deliver us from the burning fiery furnace, and he will deliver us out of thine hand, O king. But if not, be it known unto thee, O king, that we will not serve thy gods, nor worship the golden image which thou hast set up. (Daniel 3:16–18)

Oh, to God that we would have that kind of faith! And how miraculously the Lord revealed Himself to them and to the king with four men in the furnace!

Daniel remained in Babylon under the reign of Nebuchadnezzar's son King Darius because "an excellent spirit was in him." However, the king's men were jealous. They could not find fault in him (much like the trial of Jesus) and sought to attack his faith instead.

> Then this Daniel was preferred above the presidents and princes, because an excellent spirit was in him; and the king thought to set him over the whole realm. Then the presidents and princes sought to find occasion against Daniel concerning the kingdom; but they could find none occasion nor fault; forasmuch as he was faithful, neither was there any error or fault found in him. Then said these men, We shall not find any occasion against this Daniel, except we find it against him concerning the law of his God. (Daniel 6:3–5)

These wicked men played on the king's pride with the idea of a royal statue as a sole source of petitions for thirty days. "Now when Daniel knew that the writing was signed, he went into his house; and his windows being open in his chamber toward Jerusalem, he kneeled upon his knees three times a day, and prayed, and gave thanks before his God, as he did aforetime" (Daniel 6:10).

How strong was Daniel's faith and courage! He prayed openly and intentionally, not once but three times a day. What is interesting is that this was not in defiance to the king's order but rather what he did every day even before the order. He was committed to the Lord in prayer. This is in stark contrast to one who only turns to God in times of need. If someone is not already devoted to God in prayer, it will be even harder to bow when threatened.

The Christian soldier is wholeheartedly committed to the Lord. Why is it so hard for Christians to make this kind of commitment? Is it because they really do not want to let go of their worldly pleasures? Is it because they have a fear of failure or lack of courage? How can we overcome our fear? The answer is through the Holy Spirit. Stephen remained so calm when they were stoning him. He boldly glorified God in his sermon to the Jewish leaders, and for that, they killed him, as seen in Acts 7.

> When they heard these things, they were cut to the heart, and they gnashed on him with their teeth. But he, being full of the Holy Ghost, looked up stedfastly into heaven, and saw the glory of God, and Jesus standing on the right hand of God, And said, Behold, I see the heavens opened, and the Son of man standing on the right hand of God. Then they cried out with a loud voice, and stopped their ears, and ran upon him with one accord, And cast him out of the city, and stoned him: and the witnesses laid down their clothes at a young man's feet, whose name was Saul. And they stoned Stephen, calling upon God, and saying, Lord Jesus, receive my spirit. And he kneeled down, and cried with a loud voice, Lord, lay not this sin to their charge. And when he had said this, he fell asleep. (Acts 7:54–60)

What did Stephen do? He "looked up stedfastly into heaven," keeping his eyes on Jesus and calling upon God to receive his spirit. He overcame his fear through his faith in the Lord and through the power of the Holy Spirit within him, even saying the same words as Jesus, "Lay not this sin to their charge." Then "he fell asleep."

"Precious in the sight of the LORD is the death of his saints" (Psalm 116:15).

3

BE RENEWED IN THE MIND OF CHRIST PUT OFF THE DEEDS OF THE OLD MAN

Summary

Chapter 3 lays the foundation for a true Christian soldier who puts off the deeds of the old man. There is a clear parallel here to the first steps in military boot camp. They want to break you through an intense test of endurance. Similarly, the Lord breaks His people and opens their heart that the Holy Spirit may enter into the soul of man. From that point forward, there is a refining process that takes place, molding the new man into the image of God through sanctification.

A daily battle

Soldiers begin their training in boot camp, but it doesn't stop there. Each day begins with exercise and continued training in preparation for whatever mission(s) may lie ahead. No one wants to slip back into complacency.

The Lord God hath given me the tongue of
the learned, that I should know how to speak a

word in season to him that is weary: he wakeneth
morning by morning, he wakeneth mine ear to
hear as the learned. (Isaiah 50:4)

The first fight of a Christian soldier is with himself. This is the
essence of 2 Timothy 2:4: "No man that warreth entangleth *himself*
with the affairs of this life; that he may please him who hath chosen
him to be a soldier." We must not allow ourselves to be entangled in
the things of the world.

For if ye live after the flesh, ye shall die: but
if ye through the Spirit do mortify the deeds of
the body, ye shall live. (Romans 8:13)

Mortify therefore your members which are
upon the earth; fornication, uncleanness, inordi-
nate affection, evil concupiscence, and covetous-
ness, which is idolatry. (Colossians 3:5)

These are the deeds of the heathen, which we were before the
Lord saved us. As Psalm 51:5 says, "Behold, I was shapen in iniquity; and in sin did my mother conceive me." But thanks be to God,
through the death, burial, and resurrection of Jesus Christ, we who
believe are new creatures. The inward man is filled with the Holy
Spirit, ready to do God's will. However, the sinful flesh remains.
This causes a continual battle within the heart of man.

Our commitment to Christ requires sacrifice. Sacrifice requires
choice. A good soldier chooses to go into the battle even if it may cost
him his life. As Jesus says,

If any man will come after me, let him deny
himself, and take up his cross daily, and follow
me. (Luke 9:23)

And every one that hath forsaken houses, or
brethren, or sisters, or father, or mother, or wife,

or children, or lands, for my name's sake, shall receive an hundredfold, and shall inherit everlasting life. (Matthew 19:29)

Are you willing to be a living sacrifice for the Lord?

I beseech you therefore, brethren, by the mercies of God, that ye present your bodies a living sacrifice, holy, acceptable unto God, which is your reasonable service. And be not conformed to this world: but be ye transformed *by the renewing of your mind*, that ye may prove what is that good, and acceptable, and perfect, will of God. (Romans 12:1–2)

When a person joins the military, they leave everything they know behind—their home, family, and friends. They leave their comfort zone and enter into unknown territory. They submit to their superiors who now, in essence, own them. And so, we see in the Word,

For he that is called in the Lord, being a servant, is the Lord's freeman: likewise also he that is called, being free, is Christ's servant. Ye are bought with a price; be not ye the servants of men. (1 Corinthians 7:22–23)

What? know ye not that your body is the temple of the Holy Ghost which is in you, which ye have of God, and ye are not your own? For ye are bought with a price: therefore glorify God in your body, and in your spirit, which are God's. (1 Corinthians 6:19–20)

Our Lord is a jealous God, and He will not share His glory with another. We must completely submit to His authority and give Him preeminence in all things, even in the furnace of affliction.

> For my name's sake will I defer mine anger, and for my praise will I refrain for thee, that I cut thee not off. Behold, I have refined thee, but not with silver; I have chosen thee in *the furnace of affliction*. For mine own sake, even for mine own sake, will I do it: for how should my name be polluted? and *I will not give my glory unto another.* (Isaiah 48:9–11)

Those who belong to Christ are in the refiner's fire. In this life, He is refining us that we may be holy as He is holy. As we see in Isaiah 1:25, "I will turn my hand upon thee, and purely purge away thy dross, and take away all thy tin." He removes the dross to conform us into the likeness of Christ. Look at what the psalmist says in chapter 119:

> Thou hast dealt well with thy servant, O LORD, according unto thy word. Teach me good judgment and knowledge: for I have believed thy commandments. Before I was afflicted I went astray: but now have I kept thy word. Thou art good, and doest good; teach me thy statutes. The proud have forged a lie against me: but I will keep thy precepts with my whole heart. Their heart is as fat as grease; but I delight in thy law. *It is good for me that I have been afflicted; that I might learn thy statutes.* (Psalm 119:65–71)

Many people striving to be soldiers do not make it through boot camp. However, for those who do, there is a higher calling.

> For unto whomsoever much is given, of him shall be much required: and to whom men have committed much, of him they will ask the more. (Luke 12:48)

> We then that are strong ought to bear the infirmities of the weak, and not to please ourselves. (Romans 15:1)

It starts with a humble heart. We must submit to God, resist the devil, and make a concerted effort to draw nearer to God every day, as James reminds us.

> Submit yourselves therefore to God. Resist the devil, and he will flee from you. *Draw nigh to God, and he will draw nigh to you.* Cleanse your hands, ye sinners; and purify your hearts, ye double minded. Be afflicted, and mourn, and weep: let your laughter be turned to mourning, and your joy to heaviness. Humble yourselves in the sight of the Lord, and he shall lift you up. (James 4:7–10)

As new creatures in Christ, we are called into the Great Commission that others may be saved and join in the battle.

> Wherefore seeing we also are compassed about with so great a cloud of witnesses, let us lay aside every weight, and the sin which doth so easily beset us, and let us run with patience the race that is set before us. (Hebrews 12:1)

We are ambassadors for Christ:

> Therefore if any man be in Christ, he is a new creature: *old things are passed away; behold, all things are become new.* And all things are of God, who hath reconciled us to himself by Jesus Christ, and hath given to us the ministry of reconciliation; To wit, that God was in Christ, reconciling the world unto himself, not imputing their trespasses unto them; and hath committed unto us the word of reconciliation. Now then *we are ambassadors for Christ,* as though God did beseech you by us: we pray you in Christ's stead, be ye reconciled to God. (2 Corinthians 5:17–20)

The real question is, in our day-to-day lives, what does it take to be an ambassador/soldier for Christ? From my own life experience, I know that harboring feelings of resentment hindered my ability to share the light of Christ. Someone had abused me to the point that I no longer felt worthy to serve the Lord. Their presence in my day-to-day life stifled my freedom to express my feelings. I was trapped. I was in bondage. However, I did have a choice to walk away, and I made that choice because I sincerely believe that God does not want us to live in an abusive relationship, whether it is emotional, mental, or physical.

This was only half the battle, though. I remained in the bondage of an unforgiving heart. One of the things Jesus cried on the cross was "forgive them for they know not what they do." In my mind, this was different. My husband wanted to manipulate me for his own advantage, and he knew what he was doing. How could I ever forgive him for hurting me and my children?

Then the Lord reminded me. If it were not for His saving grace, I would still be living in my sins without forgiveness. The Lord's prayer in Luke 11:4 is clear: "And forgive us our sins; for we also forgive every one that is indebted to us. And lead us not into temptation; but deliver us from evil." This opened my eyes to let go of the feelings of resentment, begin the process of forgiveness, and pray for my enemies.

There are many things that hinder us in our ability to be a good soldier. Forgiveness is just one. Ruth could have remained in her sorrow and bitterness at the loss of her husband. Instead, she remained committed to her mother-in-law, Naomi:

> And Ruth said, Intreat me not to leave thee, or to return from following after thee: for whither thou goest, I will go; and where thou lodgest, I will lodge: thy people shall be my people, and thy God my God: Where thou diest, will I die, and there will I be buried: the LORD do so to me, and more also, if ought but death part thee and me. When she saw that *she was stedfastly minded* to go with her, then she left speaking unto her. (Ruth 1:16–18)

Ruth was "stedfastly minded" to do what was right in the sight of the Lord, and as a result of her faithfulness, the Lord blessed her to be in the line of David and, thus, in the line of Christ!

Being renewed in your mind means putting off the things that pull us down. Soldiers need to keep moving forward rather than dwelling in the past. The cleansing power of the Word of God is essential to a healthy mind. What do *you* need to let go of to be in the army of God?

4

BOW TO THE KING
TRUST AND OBEY

Summary

This chapter establishes the mission. A good soldier must be focused on the common goal. This requires perfect submission and obedience to their leader. For Christians, the captain of the army is Jesus Christ, King of kings and Lord of lords.

He is worthy

> Thou art worthy, O Lord, to receive glory and honour and power: for thou hast created all things, and for thy pleasure they are and were created. (Revelation 4:11)

> Worthy is the Lamb that was slain to receive power, and riches, and wisdom, and strength, and honour, and glory, and blessing. (Revelation 5:12)

The Lord God Almighty is worthy of all praise, honor, and glory. This is His creation. He is the great shepherd, and we are the sheep of His pasture. Our whole goal in life should be to honor God, who is the Father, Son, and Holy Spirit. This is the primary theme throughout the whole Bible. The following scriptures declare the oneness of the Godhead, to whom every knee shall bow:

> I have sworn by myself, the word is gone out of my mouth in righteousness, and shall not return, That unto me every knee shall bow, every tongue shall swear. (Isaiah 45:23)

> For it is written, As I live, saith the Lord, every knee shall bow to me, and every tongue shall confess to God. (Romans 14:11)

> That at the name of Jesus every knee should bow, of things in heaven, and things in earth, and things under the earth. (Philippians 2:10)

The Lord says in Isaiah 45:23 that every knee shall bow to Him; in Romans, that every knee shall bow to God; and in Philippians, that every knee should bow to Jesus. So "who is this King of glory? The LORD strong and mighty, the LORD mighty in battle" (Psalm 24:8).

We serve one God, the true and living God, who is the Father, Son, and Holy Spirit. "For in Him dwelleth the fullness of the Godhead bodily" (Colossians 2:9), and He is the One who is mighty in battle. Our job is to honor Him, trust Him, and obey Him. Obedience is essential. The army of God must march in unison. Internal strife or any kind of rebellion hinders the forward movement. A chain is no stronger than its weakest link. As the Lord says, "Honour all men. Love the brotherhood. Fear God. Honour the king" (1 Peter 2:17). A great lesson can be learned from the battle at Ai in Joshua 7. The army of God must destroy the accursed thing from within to be able to have the victory.

> But the children of Israel committed a trespass in the accursed thing: for Achan, the son

of Carmi, the son of Zabdi, the son of Zerah, of
the tribe of Judah, took of the accursed thing:
and the anger of the LORD was kindled against
the children of Israel. And Joshua sent men from
Jericho to Ai, which is beside Bethaven, on the
east side of Bethel, and spake unto them, saying, Go up and view the country. And the men
went up and viewed Ai. And they returned to
Joshua, and said unto him, Let not all the people
go up; but let about two or three thousand men
go up and smite Ai; and make not all the people
to labour thither; for they are but few. So there
went up thither of the people about three thousand men: and they fled before the men of Ai.
And the men of Ai smote of them about thirty
and six men: for they chased them from before
the gate even unto Shebarim, and smote them in
the going down: wherefore the hearts of the people melted, and became as water. And Joshua rent
his clothes, and fell to the earth upon his face
before the ark of the LORD until the eventide, he
and the elders of Israel, and put dust upon their
heads. (Joshua 7:1–6)

And Joshua said, Alas, O Lord God,
wherefore hast thou at all brought this people
over Jordan, to deliver us into the hand of the
Amorites, to destroy us? would to God we had
been content, and dwelt on the other side Jordan!
O Lord, what shall I say, when Israel turneth their
backs before their enemies! For the Canaanites
and all the inhabitants of the land shall hear of
it, and shall environ us round, and cut off our
name from the earth: and what wilt thou do unto
thy great name? And the LORD said unto Joshua,
Get thee up; wherefore liest thou thus upon thy

> face? Israel hath sinned, and they have also trans-
> gressed my covenant which I commanded them:
> for they have even taken of the accursed thing,
> and have also stolen, and dissembled also, and
> they have put it even among their own stuff.
> (Joshua 7:7–11)

> Therefore the children of Israel could not
> stand before their enemies, but turned their backs
> before their enemies, because they were accursed:
> neither will I be with you any more, except ye
> destroy the accursed from among you. Up, sanc-
> tify the people, and say, Sanctify yourselves
> against tomorrow: for thus saith the LORD God
> of Israel, There is an accursed thing in the midst
> of thee, O Israel: thou canst not stand before
> thine enemies, until ye take away the accursed
> thing from among you. (Joshua 7:12–13)

The battle is the Lord's, but He requires our obedience. One of the important responsibilities of the local church is to discipline those who might have a rebellious spirit. This is a cleansing process, holding the members accountable for the love of the brethren. The Lord will use a faithful church to accomplish His victory in each battle that may arise. The *assembly* must remember, however, that the battle is the Lord's, as seen in 1 Samuel 17:47: "And all this assembly shall know that the LORD saveth not with sword and spear: for the battle is the LORD's, and he will give you into our hands."

This also was true in the life of King Jehoshaphat, as seen in 2 Chronicles 20:15:

> And he said, Hearken ye, all Judah, and
> ye inhabitants of Jerusalem, and thou king
> Jehoshaphat, Thus saith the LORD unto you, Be
> not afraid nor dismayed by reason of this great
> multitude; for the battle is not yours, but God's.

We trust in the holiness of God and His perfect righteousness. Our hope is in the fullness of His light to overcome evil and dispel all of the darkness. We are learning all about the knowledge of good and evil, just as God said in the Garden of Eden. And we know that the end of the curse is eternal death and hell without the salvation of our Lord Jesus Christ. We bow to Him because He is God, and there is none other.

What did Thomas do when Christ told him to touch His hands and His side (John 20:27)? What did Stephen do when they were stoning him to death (Acts 7:59)? What did Paul do when Christ appeared to him on the road to Damascus (Acts 9:4)?

Paul bowed to Jesus and committed himself to His service, as he says in Philippians 3:10,

> That I may know him, and the power of his resurrection, and the fellowship of his sufferings, being made conformable unto his death; If by any means I might attain unto the resurrection of the dead.

And Paul wanted his brothers and sisters in Christ to do the same, as seen in Ephesians 3.

> Wherefore I desire that ye faint not at my tribulations for you, which is your glory. For this cause I bow my knees unto the Father of our Lord Jesus Christ, Of whom the whole family in heaven and earth is named, That he would grant you, according to the riches of his glory, to be strengthened with might by his Spirit in the inner man; That Christ may dwell in your hearts by faith; that ye, being rooted and grounded in love, May be able to comprehend with all saints what is the breadth, and length, and depth, and height; And to know the love of Christ, which passeth knowledge, that ye might be filled with

all the fulness of God. Now unto him that is able to do exceeding abundantly above all that we ask or think, according to the power that worketh in us, Unto him be glory in the church by Christ Jesus throughout all ages, world without end. Amen. (Ephesians 3:13–21)

We bow to God because we love Him. "We love him, because he first loved us" (1 John 4:19). And if we love Him, we want to obey Him. Matthew 22 reminds us of the two greatest commandments:

Jesus said unto him, Thou shalt love the Lord thy God with all thy heart, and with all thy soul, and with all thy mind. This is the first and great commandment. And the second is like unto it, Thou shalt love thy neighbour as thyself. On these two commandments hang all the law and the prophets. (Matthew 22:37–40)

A military recruit is useless if he is not willing to submit to his superiors. A Christian soldier cannot serve God unless he bows to Him. Psalm 95 reminds us that He is worthy of all our worship and praise:

O come, let us sing unto the Lord: let us make a joyful noise to the rock of our salvation. Let us come before his presence with thanks-giving, and make a joyful noise unto him with psalms. For the Lord is a great God, and a great King above all gods. In his hand are the deep places of the earth: the strength of the hills is his also. The sea is his, and he made it: and his hands formed the dry land. *O come, let us worship and bow down: let us kneel before the* Lord *our maker.* For he is our God; and we are the people of his pasture, and the sheep of his hand. To day if ye

will hear his voice, Harden not your heart, as in
the provocation, and as in the day of temptation
in the wilderness: When your fathers tempted
me, proved me, and saw my work. Forty years
long was I grieved with this generation, and said,
It is a people that do err in their heart, and they
have not known my ways: Unto whom I sware in
my wrath that they should not enter into my rest.

5

Practice Discipline and Training Work Out Your Own Salvation with Fear and Trembling

Summary

This chapter deals with the importance of discipline and training. A good soldier must work every day to exercise body, mind, and spirit. Likewise, a good Christian must strive to work out their own salvation with fear and trembling. As James says, "Faith without works is dead." Faith requires action. When a soldier puts what he's learned into action, he builds strength and confidence.

A matter of discipline

Philippians 2:12 is not about working for salvation but rather working out what the Lord has worked within.

For by grace are ye saved through faith; and
that not of yourselves: it is the gift of God: not

of works, lest any man should boast. (Ephesians 2:8)

Wherefore, my beloved, as ye have always obeyed, not as in my presence only, but now much more in my absence, work out your own salvation with fear and trembling. (Philippians 2:12)

This requires the nurturing of body, mind, and spirit. The body needs healthy nutrition and exercise. The mind needs the Word of God, precept upon precept. The spirit needs wisdom, encouragement, and sincere fellowship. This is found in the Lord's true churches.

Church discipline is predicated on the self-discipline of the members. A good Christian soldier practices self-discipline to maintain a state of readiness, as God may call him into the battle. So it is most certainly true that the Lord may use a faithful individual, a faithful group of believers, and a faithful church to accomplish His holy purpose.

The soldier must respect his captain's authority, trusting in his leadership to fulfill the mission. The brethren must respect their pastor's authority, trusting in his leadership to fulfill the great commission. "Touch not my anointed," the Lord says, honoring his chosen shepherd of the flock of God. "Obey them that have the rule over you, and submit yourselves: for they watch for your souls, as they that must give account, that they may do it with joy, and not with grief: for that is unprofitable for you" (Hebrews 13:17).

The Lord has His bit in our mouth. He trieth the reins to bring us into perfect submission to do His will. He breaks us and then trains us to obey His commands, just like a horse is tamed and trained and just like a soldier is broken in boot camp and trained for battle. James gives a good analogy.

My brethren, be not many masters, knowing that we shall receive the greater condemnation. For in many things we offend all. If any man offend not in word, the same is a perfect man, and able also to bridle the whole body. Behold, we put bits in the horses' mouths, that they may obey us; and we turn about their whole body. Behold also the ships, which though they be so great, and are driven of fierce winds, yet are they turned about with a very small helm, whithersoever the governor listeth. Even so the tongue is a little member, and boasteth great things. Behold, how great a matter a little fire kindleth! (James 3:1–5)

The Lord wants us to control our tongue as well as all our thoughts and actions. "And whatsoever ye do in word or deed, do all in the name of the Lord Jesus, giving thanks to God and the Father by him" (Colossians 3:17). The following verses bring comfort, knowing that the Lord is trying our reins:

I the LORD search the heart, I try the reins, even to give every man according to his ways, and according to the fruit of his doings. (Jeremiah 17:10)

Examine me, O LORD, and prove me; try my reins and my heart. (Psalm 26:2)

But, O LORD of hosts, that triest the righteous, and seest the reins and the heart, let me see thy vengeance on them: for unto thee have I opened my cause. (Jeremiah 20:12)

Oh let the wickedness of the wicked come to an end; but establish the just: for the righteous God trieth the hearts and reins. (Psalm 7:9)

Keep your emotions in check

One of the pitfalls of a highly trained soldier can be uncontrolled aggression. After all, we are training for battle. Human emotions can interfere in one's ability to react in a proper manner. It is critical that the soldier not step out of the will of God. "For the wrath of man worketh not the righteousness of God" (James 1:20).

Self-control is most often hindered by human emotions. Ephesians 4:26 says, "Be ye angry, and sin not: let not the sun go down upon your wrath." The Lord allows His children to experience trials to build strength and stamina. A combat veteran is prepared for the front line. A combat Christian is ready to withstand the wiles of the devil. He does not allow emotions to weaken his stand for Christ. He knows how to rise above the situations, how to be centered in Christ and not allow himself to be frustrated, annoyed, or anxious. This gives him a clear mind, courage, and confidence, knowing that the Lord "hath raised us up together, and made us sit together in heavenly places in Christ Jesus" (Ephesians 2:6).

A good soldier seeks to follow the right instructions, and for a Christian, that is most certainly the Bible.

> All scripture is given by inspiration of God, and is profitable for doctrine, for reproof, for correction, for instruction in righteousness. (2 Timothy 3:16)

> The fear of the LORD is the instruction of wisdom; and before honour is humility. (Proverbs 15:33)

It is not just a matter of reading the Word but also studying, as Paul declares to Timothy:

> Study to shew thyself approved unto God, a workman that needeth not to be ashamed, rightly dividing the word of truth. But shun profane and

vain babblings: for they will increase unto more ungodliness. (2 Timothy 2:15–16)

Psalm 119 is all about the eternal value of the Word of God. As we read in verse 11, "Thy word have I hid in mine heart, that I might not sin against thee." And "whosoever is born of God doth not commit sin; for his seed remaineth in him: and he cannot sin, because he is born of God" (1 John 3:9). We are not to be pulled away by "doubtful disputations" (Romans 14:1).

Avoid distractions

A believer who is grounded in the Word of God is ready to be trained as a soldier for Christ. A well-trained soldier knows how to maintain situational awareness. This requires attention to everything going on around you without distraction. The enemy knows our weaknesses. If he can pull us off course into diversions, he can win the battle. First Timothy emphasizes that we are to discern the spirits.

> Now the Spirit speaketh expressly, that in the latter times some shall depart from the faith, giving heed to seducing spirits, and doctrines of devils; Speaking lies in hypocrisy; having their conscience seared with a hot iron; Forbidding to marry, and commanding to abstain from meats, which God hath created to be received with thanksgiving of them which believe and know the truth. For every creature of God is good, and nothing to be refused, if it be received with thanksgiving: For it is sanctified by the word of God and prayer. If thou put the brethren in remembrance of these things, thou shalt be a good minister of Jesus Christ, nourished up in the words of faith and of good doctrine, whereunto thou hast attained. But refuse profane and

old wives' fables, and exercise thyself rather unto godliness. For bodily exercise profiteth little: but godliness is profitable unto all things, having promise of the life that now is, and of that which is to come. This is a faithful saying and worthy of all acceptation. For therefore we both labour and suffer reproach, because we trust in the living God, who is the Saviour of all men, specially of those that believe. These things command and teach. (1 Timothy 4:1–11)

The battle is on every front. We can be hindered by our own sins, as well as the sins of others. It is important not to be drawn into the drama that entraps even the brethren. As Ephesians 5:12 says, "It is a shame even to speak of those things which are done of them in secret." We want to have compassion but also be cautious not to darken our own spirit. As Matthew 7:6 says, "Give not that which is holy unto the dogs, neither cast ye your pearls before swine, lest they trample them under their feet, and turn again and rend you."

We can be drawn away by our own lusts as well. It is a daily exercise to "lay aside every weight, and the sin which doth so easily beset us" (Hebrews 12:1). We are to "love not the world, neither the things that are in the world. If any man love the world, the love of the Father is not in him" (1 John 2:15).

Don't be caught in the devil's traps. He wants us to be entangled in the world, in superstitions, in delusions, in other things that cause confusion and doubt. As James 1:8 says, "A double minded man is unstable in all his ways." Moreover, "be sober, be vigilant; because your adversary the devil, as a roaring lion, walketh about, seeking whom he may devour" (1 Peter 5:8). As Ephesians 4:30 says, "Grieve not the holy Spirit of God, whereby ye are sealed unto the day of redemption." The Bible teaches not to eat the communion without repentance. Neither should we go into battle without the Holy Spirit. This is personal responsibility.

The importance of wisdom

The prerequisite for discipline and training is wisdom. "The fear of the LORD is the beginning of wisdom: and the knowledge of the holy is understanding" (Proverbs 9:10). An ignorant soldier is useless. "His watchmen are blind: they are all ignorant, they are all dumb dogs, they cannot bark; sleeping, lying down, loving to slumber" (Isaiah 56:10). A wise Christian soldier is a jewel in the crown of the Lord. James, in chapter 3, gives a clear contrast.

> Who is a wise man and endued with knowledge among you? let him shew out of a good conversation his works with meekness of wisdom. But if ye have bitter envying and strife in your hearts, glory not, and lie not against the truth. This wisdom descendeth not from above, but is earthly, sensual, devilish. For where envying and strife is, there is confusion and every evil work. But the wisdom that is from above is first pure, then peaceable, gentle, and easy to be intreated, full of mercy and good fruits, without partiality, and without hypocrisy. And the fruit of righteousness is sown in peace of them that make peace. (James 3:13–18)

"Wisdom is the principal thing; therefore get wisdom: and with all thy getting get understanding" (Proverbs 4:7). Don't let the things of this world complicate the simplicity of Christ. "For God is not the author of confusion" (1 Corinthians 14:33). And we know that "the wisdom of this world is foolishness with God. For it is written, He taketh the wise in their own craftiness" (1 Corinthians 3:19). If we desire the wisdom of God, all we have to do is ask, as James 1:5 says, "If any of you lack wisdom, let him ask of God, that giveth to all men liberally, and upbraideth not; and it shall be given him."

The Lord answers clearly in Ephesians 1:17, "That the God of our Lord Jesus Christ, the Father of glory, may give unto you the spirit of wisdom and revelation in *the knowledge of him*."

A good soldier is steady, dependable, even-tempered, not easily shaken. A good Christian soldier is not easily "tossed to and fro, and carried about with every wind of doctrine" (Ephesians 4:14). This comes from a strong faith that is based on an understanding of the truth. As we see in Isaiah 33:6, "and wisdom and knowledge shall be *the stability of thy times*, and strength of salvation: the fear of the LORD is his treasure." The following scriptures emphasize the importance of wisdom:

> For the LORD giveth wisdom: out of his mouth cometh knowledge and understanding. (Proverbs 2:6)

> The fear of the LORD is the instruction of wisdom; and before honour is humility. (Proverbs 15:33)

> Wisdom is better than weapons of war: but one sinner destroyeth much good. (Ecclesiastes 9:18)

> For wisdom is a defence, and money is a defence: but the excellency of knowledge is, that wisdom giveth life to them that have it. (Ecclesiastes 7:12)

> Wisdom strengtheneth the wise more than ten mighty men which are in the city. (Ecclesiastes 7:19)

> Happy is the man that findeth wisdom, and the man that getteth understanding. For the merchandise of it is better than the merchandise

of silver, and the gain thereof than fine gold. She is more precious than rubies: and all the things thou canst desire are not to be compared unto her. Length of days is in her right hand; and in her left hand riches and honour. Her ways are ways of pleasantness, and all her paths are peace. She is a tree of life to them that lay hold upon her: and happy is every one that retaineth her. The LORD by wisdom hath founded the earth; by understanding hath he established the heavens. By his knowledge the depths are broken up, and the clouds drop down the dew. My son, let not them depart from thine eyes: keep sound wisdom and discretion: So shall they be life unto thy soul, and grace to thy neck. Then shalt thou walk in thy way safely, and thy foot shall not stumble. When thou liest down, thou shalt not be afraid: yea, thou shalt lie down, and thy sleep shall be sweet. Be not afraid of sudden fear, neither of the desolation of the wicked, when it cometh. For the LORD shall be thy confidence, and shall keep thy foot from being taken. (Proverbs 3:13–26)

Manage your resources well

A good soldier is a good steward over his resources. He uses his resources wisely and is faithful in tithing. A military soldier maintains his equipment and ensures adequate supply at all times. Think of the ten virgins. "They that were foolish took their lamps, and took no oil with them: But the wise took oil in their vessels with their lamps" (Matthew 25:3–4).

The oil represents the Holy Spirit, whom only God can give. Sadly, the foolish were unconcerned about their empty lamps until it was too late, and then they wanted to take oil from the wise. The foolish were more concerned about the pleasures of this world than the treasures of Heaven. As 1 Timothy 6:10 says, "the love of money is the root of all evil."

> *But godliness with contentment is great gain.* For we brought nothing into this world, and it is certain we can carry nothing out. And having food and raiment let us be therewith content. But they that will be rich fall into temptation and a snare, and into many foolish and hurtful lusts, which drown men in destruction and perdition. *For the love of money is the root of all evil*: which while some coveted after, they have erred from the faith, and pierced themselves through with many sorrows. But thou, O man of God, flee these things; and follow after righteousness, godliness, faith, love, patience, meekness. (1 Timothy 6:6–11)

We have everything we need in the Lord. He has provided the "sure mercies of David"—His everlasting covenant, His promises, and His love. We must make a concerted effort to discipline ourselves, letting go of the things that hinder our ability to serve Him. We should want to honor Him with our lives, for He is our "leader and commander," as seen in Isaiah 55.

> Ho, every one that thirsteth, come ye to the waters, and he that hath no money; come ye, buy, and eat; yea, come, buy wine and milk without money and without price. *Wherefore do ye spend money for that which is not bread?* and your labour for that which satisfieth not? hearken diligently unto me, and eat ye that which is good, and let your soul delight itself in fatness. Incline your ear, and come unto me: hear, and your soul shall live; and I will make an everlasting covenant with you, even *the sure mercies of David*. Behold,

I have given him for a witness to the people, *a leader and commander to the people*. Behold, thou shalt call a nation that thou knowest not, and nations that knew not thee shall run unto thee because of the Lord thy God, and for the Holy One of Israel; for he hath glorified thee. Seek ye the Lord while he may be found, call ye upon him while he is near: Let the wicked forsake his way, and the unrighteous man his thoughts: and let him return unto the Lord, and he will have mercy upon him; and to our God, for he will abundantly pardon. For my thoughts are not your thoughts, neither are your ways my ways, saith the Lord. (Isaiah 55:1–8)

For as the heavens are higher than the earth, so are my ways higher than your ways, and my thoughts than your thoughts. For as the rain cometh down, and the snow from heaven, and returneth not thither, but watereth the earth, and maketh it bring forth and bud, that it may give seed to the sower, and bread to the eater: So shall my word be that goeth forth out of my mouth: it shall not return unto me void, but it shall accomplish that which I please, and it shall prosper in the thing whereto I sent it. For ye shall go out with joy, and be led forth with peace: the mountains and the hills shall break forth before you into singing, and all the trees of the field shall clap their hands. Instead of the thorn shall come up the fir tree, and instead of the brier shall come up the myrtle tree: and it shall be to the Lord for a name, for an everlasting sign that shall not be cut off. (Isaiah 55:9–13)

Remain determined

Ongoing discipline and training require passion, commitment, and determination. We will not continue the *regiment* unless there is sincere belief in the mission—the mark of the high calling. As Philippians 3:14 says, "I press toward the mark for the prize of the high calling of God in Christ Jesus." We continue in the faith because we love the Lord and His people. Philippians 4 puts the *regiment* in simple terms.

> Rejoice in the Lord alway: and again I say, Rejoice. Let your moderation be known unto all men. The Lord is at hand. Be careful for nothing; but in every thing by prayer and supplication with thanksgiving let your requests be made known unto God. And the peace of God, which passeth all understanding, shall keep your hearts and minds through Christ Jesus. Finally, brethren, whatsoever things are true, whatsoever things are honest, whatsoever things are just, whatsoever things are pure, whatsoever things are lovely, whatsoever things are of good report; if there be any virtue, and if there be any praise, think on these things. (Philippians 4:4–8)

Discipline and training are an ongoing work that requires personal responsibility. However, the true Christian soldier knows that they are nothing without the Lord. As King David says in Psalm 144:1, "Blessed be the LORD my strength, which teacheth my hands to war, and my fingers to fight." We are in a war, and we need to stand fast, watch, and pray. "Watch ye therefore, and pray always, that ye may be accounted worthy to escape all these things that shall come to pass, and to stand before the Son of man" (Luke 21:36).

6

Know the Enemy Watch and Pray

Summary

This chapter is critical to the "battle plan." The first step is to know the enemy.

> Be sober, be vigilant; because your adversary the devil, as a roaring lion, walketh about, seeking whom he may devour. (1 Peter 5:8)

> For we wrestle not against flesh and blood, but against principalities, against powers, against the rulers of the darkness of this world, against spiritual wickedness in high places. (Ephesians 6:12)

A strong Christian soldier must prepare for battle, strategize when to fight, practice patience in persecution, and stand strong against the enemy. The first question we have to ask is, who is the enemy? It is the wickedness of Satan, sin, and self.

Who is the enemy?

The devil loves *me, myself,* and *I.* He loves sin. His evil plan started in the Garden of Eden with deceitful lies that enticed Adam and Eve. Those who dwell in sin serve their father, the devil, and "he that committeth sin is of the devil; for the devil sinneth from the beginning. For this purpose the Son of God was manifested, that he might destroy the works of the devil" (1 John 3:8).

The battle began in the spiritual realm, as we see in Luke 10:18, which says, "And he said unto them, I beheld Satan as lightning fall from heaven." He is the god of this fallen world (2 Corinthians 4:4), and he desires to sift us as wheat (Luke 22:31). "For, lo, they lie in wait for my soul: the mighty are gathered against me; not for my transgression, nor for my sin, O Lord" (Psalm 59:3). The wicked "loved darkness rather than light, because their deeds were evil" (John 3:19). They are born speaking lies, as we read in Psalms.

> The wicked are estranged from the womb:
> they go astray as soon as they be born, speaking
> lies. Their poison is like the poison of a serpent:
> they are like the deaf adder that stoppeth her ear;
> Which will not hearken to the voice of charmers,
> charming never so wisely. (Psalm 58:3–5)

The enemy is mean and very ugly. His actions are extremely grotesque, so is war. Soldiers must learn how to control their thoughts and feelings with the inevitable atrocities of war.

There is no escape and there is no turning back. As seen in Matthew 13, the wheat and the tares must grow up together, and the tares are getting very big and very ugly. When all around is darkness, the Christian soldier stands firm in the light of the Lord, even if unto death. "Precious in the sight of the Lord is the death of his saints" (Psalm 116:15).

Satan's tactics are broad and diverse. He is behind all idolatry, which is the worship of anything that is not God. It is rebellion against God, as seen in 1 Samuel, where the prophet Samuel warns King Saul against idolatry and witchcraft.

> And the LORD sent thee on a journey, and said, Go and utterly destroy the sinners the Amalekites, and fight against them until they be consumed. Wherefore then didst thou not obey the voice of the LORD, but didst fly upon the spoil, and didst evil in the sight of the LORD? And Saul said unto Samuel, Yea, I have obeyed the voice of the LORD, and have gone the way which the LORD sent me, and have brought Agag the king of Amalek, and have utterly destroyed the Amalekites. But the people took of the spoil, sheep and oxen, the chief of the things which should have been utterly destroyed, to sacrifice unto the LORD thy God in Gilgal. And Samuel said, Hath the LORD as great delight in burnt offerings and sacrifices, as in obeying the voice of the LORD? Behold, to obey is better than sacrifice, and to hearken than the fat of rams. For rebellion is as the sin of witchcraft, and stubbornness is as iniquity and idolatry. Because thou hast rejected the word of the LORD, he hath also rejected thee from being king. And Saul said unto Samuel, I have sinned: for I have transgressed the commandment of the LORD, and thy words: *because I feared the people, and obeyed their voice.* Now therefore, I pray thee, pardon my sin, and turn again with me, that I may worship the LORD. And Samuel said unto Saul, I will not return with thee: for thou hast rejected the word of the LORD, and the LORD hath rejected thee from being king over Israel. (1 Samuel 15:18–26)

King Saul feared the people more than he feared the Lord. That is one of Satan's favorite evil tactics. We are social creatures who have a great desire to be accepted by others. This would be especially important for a king, desiring the approval of his kingdom. It is very important that we not succumb to societal pressures. The world is traveling down a broad path that leads to destruction. We are on the narrow path that leads to life everlasting.

The earthly realm is full of enticements, and mankind is never satisfied. "For all that is in the world, the lust of the flesh, and the lust of the eyes, and the pride of life, is not of the Father, but is of the world" (1 John 2:16). Mankind lusts for stimulation. They desire something more, consume it, and then desire more. In Sodom and Gomorrah, they were always looking for "fresh meat" and more ways of perversion. People find pleasure in sorcery and seduction. They play with fire and get burned. They curse God and are ultimately cast into the lake of fire.

Satan has many temptations in his bag of tricks. They are the works of the flesh, which are overcome if we walk in the Spirit, as Paul proclaims in Galatians,

> This I say then, Walk in the Spirit, and ye shall not fulfil the lust of the flesh. For the flesh lusteth against the Spirit, and the Spirit against the flesh: and these are contrary the one to the other: so that ye cannot do the things that ye would. But if ye be led of the Spirit, ye are not under the law. Now the works of the flesh are manifest, which are these; Adultery, fornication, uncleanness, lasciviousness, Idolatry, witchcraft, hatred, variance, emulations, wrath, strife, seditions, heresies, Envyings, murders, drunkenness, revellings, and such like: of the which I tell you before, as I have also told you in time past, that they which do such things shall not inherit the kingdom of God. (Galatians 5:16–21)

The Christian soldier must walk in the Spirit and not fulfill the lust of the flesh. Our fleshly desires come from our love for the things of the world, as John warns,

> Love not the world, neither the things that are in the world. If any man love the world, the love of the Father is not in him. For all that is in the world, the lust of the flesh, and the lust of the eyes, and the pride of life, is not of the Father, but is of the world. And the world passeth away, and the lust thereof: but he that doeth the will of God abideth for ever. *Little children, it is the last time: and as ye have heard that antichrist shall come, even now are there many antichrists; whereby we know that it is the last time.* They went out from us, but they were not of us; for if they had been of us, they would no doubt have continued with us: but they went out, that they might be made manifest that they were not all of us. But ye have an unction from the Holy One, and ye know all things. (1 John 2:15–20)

Isn't it interesting to see how the Lord moves from talking about the lust of the flesh to the Antichrist? The affairs of this world draw many people down that broad path.

> Enter ye in at the strait gate: for wide is the gate, and broad is the way, that leadeth to destruction, and many there be which go in thereat: Because strait is the gate, and narrow is the way, which leadeth unto life, and few there be that find it. Beware of false prophets, which come to you in sheep's clothing, but inwardly they are ravening wolves. (Matthew 7:13–15)

The evil one is preparing the way for the coming of the abomination of desolation we read about in Matthew 24. Many will be gathered around the temple in those days when Satan will reveal his true nature. Until that day, Satan manifests himself in false apostles, deceitful workers, and even as an angel of light, as seen in 2 Corinthians.

> For such are false apostles, deceitful workers, transforming themselves into the apostles of Christ. And no marvel; for Satan himself is transformed into an angel of light. Therefore it is no great thing if his ministers also be transformed as the ministers of righteousness; whose end shall be according to their works. (2 Corinthians 11:13–15)

This knowledge should cause God's children to be on guard and careful to discern the spirits because "ye have an unction from the Holy One, and ye know all things" (1 John 2:20). Christian soldiers do not want to align themselves with so-called allies who may be enemies. There are many *megachurches* today that draw in multitudes with modern music and motivational speeches, only seeking to please the crowd of "itching ears," as 2 Timothy proclaims,

> For the time will come when they will not endure sound doctrine; but after their own lusts shall they heap to themselves teachers, having itching ears; And they shall turn away their ears from the truth, and shall be turned unto fables. But watch thou in all things, endure afflictions, do the work of an evangelist, make full proof of thy ministry. (2 Timothy 4:3–5)

Satan's demonic influence infects those who succumb to his temptations. They follow man's rituals and traditions rather than God's Word.

> Now the Spirit speaketh expressly, that in the latter times some shall depart from the faith, giving heed to seducing spirits, and doctrines of devils; Speaking lies in hypocrisy; having their conscience seared with a hot iron; Forbidding to marry, and commanding to abstain from meats, which God hath created to be received with thanksgiving of them which believe and know the truth. (1 Timothy 4:1–3)

As Psalm 1 says, "Blessed is the man that walketh not in the counsel of the ungodly, nor standeth in the way of sinners, nor sitteth in the seat of the scornful." It is better to turn them over to Satan, for their wickedness will come upon their own heads, as 2 Peter explains,

> But chiefly them that walk after the flesh in the lust of uncleanness, and despise government. Presumptuous are they, selfwilled, they are not afraid to speak evil of dignities. Whereas angels, which are greater in power and might, bring not railing accusation against them before the Lord. But these, as natural brute beasts, made to be taken and destroyed, speak evil of the things that they understand not; and shall utterly perish in their own corruption; And shall receive the reward of unrighteousness, as *they that count it pleasure to riot in the day time.* Spots they are and blemishes, sporting themselves with their own deceivings while they feast with you; Having eyes full of adultery, and that cannot cease from sin; beguiling unstable souls: an heart they have exercised with covetous practices; cursed children:

Which have forsaken the right way, and are gone astray, following the way of Balaam the son of Bosor, who loved the wages of unrighteousness; But was rebuked for his iniquity: the dumb ass speaking with man's voice forbad the madness of the prophet. (2 Peter 2:10–16)

These are wells without water, clouds that are carried with a tempest; to whom the mist of darkness is reserved for ever. For when they speak great swelling words of vanity, they allure through the lusts of the flesh, through much wantonness, those that were clean escaped from them who live in error. *While they promise them liberty, they themselves are the servants of corruption: for of whom a man is overcome, of the same is he brought in bondage.* For if after they have escaped the pollutions of the world through the knowledge of the Lord and Saviour Jesus Christ, they are again entangled therein, and overcome, the latter end is worse with them than the beginning. For it had been better for them not to have known the way of righteousness, than, after they have known it, to turn from the holy commandment delivered unto them. But it is happened unto them according to the true proverb, The dog is turned to his own vomit again; and the sow that was washed to her wallowing in the mire. (2 Peter 2:17–22)

Just as one can know a Christian by the fruit of his labor, so can one know the wicked by his rotten fruit. "The wicked walk on every side, when the vilest men are exalted" (Psalm 12:8). As the days grow darker and sin abounds, their true identities will be revealed. Remember what 2 Thessalonians 2:3 says, "Let no man deceive you by any means: for that day shall not come, except there come a falling away first, and that man of sin be revealed, the son of perdition." The

Lord warns His people of the depths of sin that will pervade mankind, including homosexuality. They worship the creation rather than the Creator, as seen in Romans.

> For this cause God gave them up unto vile affections: for even their women did change the natural use into that which is against nature: And likewise also the men, leaving the natural use of the woman, burned in their lust one toward another; men with men working that which is unseemly, and receiving in themselves that recompence of their error which was meet. And even as they did not like to retain God in their knowledge, God gave them over to a reprobate mind, to do those things which are not convenient; Being filled with all unrighteousness, fornication, wickedness, covetousness, maliciousness; full of envy, murder, debate, deceit, malignity; whisperers, Backbiters, haters of God, despiteful, proud, boasters, inventors of evil things, disobedient to parents, Without understanding, covenantbreakers, without natural affection, implacable, unmerciful: Who knowing the judgment of God, that they which commit such things are worthy of death, not only do the same, but have pleasure in them that do them. (Romans 1:26–32)

It is good to pause at this point and consider this particular battle. Homosexuality is one of the most contentious issues of this time in history. Yes, Christians believe it is a sin. However, Christians must confess that they also sin. If it were not for the grace of God, we would be on our way to hell. The question is, should we fight this battle or keep the door open to share the gospel?

I have an acquaintance who is gay. We only see each other on occasion, but each time is pleasant. He knows that I am a Christian who believes that his lifestyle is not according to God's Word. I have shared with him some of my shortcomings as well, and we have a bond of forgiveness. This kind of love gives me opportunities to share stories from the Bible about Christ's life, His teachings, His sacrifice, and His resurrection power. Doesn't this make us think that maybe we should pick our battles?

Potential pitfalls

The Christian soldier must be careful not to fall into Satan's traps. First John 4 gives clear instruction on how to try the spirits. Do they believe that Jesus is God? If not, they have the spirit of Antichrist. If not, they are the children of their father, the devil (John 8:44).

> Beloved, believe not every spirit, but try the spirits whether they are of God: because many false prophets are gone out into the world. Hereby know ye the Spirit of God: Every spirit that confesseth that Jesus Christ is come in the flesh is of God: And every spirit that confesseth not that Jesus Christ is come in the flesh is not of God: and this is that spirit of antichrist, whereof ye have heard that it should come; and even now already is it in the world. (1 John 4:1–3)

The enemy is out there, but he also is within us. Satan cannot possess the children of God, but he can hinder them. We also can hinder ourselves. We can be our own worst enemy. Sin begins with selfish desires and rebellion against God.

> But every man is tempted, when he is drawn away of his own lust, and enticed. Then when lust hath conceived, it bringeth forth sin: and sin, when it is finished, bringeth forth death. (James 1:14–15)

If we say that we have no sin, we deceive ourselves, and the truth is not in us. (1 John 1:8)

Let not sin therefore reign in your mortal body, that ye should obey it in the lusts thereof. Neither yield ye your members as instruments of unrighteousness unto sin: but yield yourselves unto God, as those that are alive from the dead, and your members as instruments of righteousness unto God. (Romans 6:12–13)

Know ye not, that to whom ye yield yourselves servants to obey, his servants ye are to whom ye obey; whether of sin unto death, or of obedience unto righteousness? (Romans 6:16)

Sin incapacitates us. Listen to what David says in Psalm 38:3: "There is no soundness in my flesh because of thine anger; neither is there any rest in my bones because of my sin." Sin manifests itself in pride, and "pride goeth before destruction, and an haughty spirit before a fall" (Proverbs 16:18). "An high look, and a proud heart, and the plowing of the wicked, is sin" (Proverbs 21:4).

God hates sin

There is a full-size billboard on the interstate in my city that says, "God is not angry." This is far from the truth. "God judgeth the righteous, and God is angry with the wicked every day" (Psalm 7:11).

A naughty person, a wicked man, walketh with a froward mouth. He winketh with his eyes, he speaketh with his feet, he teacheth with his fingers; Frowardness is in his heart, he deviseth mischief continually; he soweth discord. Therefore shall his calamity come suddenly; suddenly shall he be broken without remedy. *These six things doth the* LORD *hate: yea, seven are an abomination unto him*: A proud look, a lying tongue, and hands that shed innocent blood, An heart that deviseth wicked imaginations, feet that be swift in running to mischief, A false witness that speaketh lies, and he that soweth discord among brethren. (Proverbs 6:12–19)

If the Lord hates sin, shouldn't we?

Psalm 139:21 says, "Do not I hate them, O LORD, that hate thee? and am not I grieved with those that rise up against thee?" We must remember that "the fear of the LORD is to hate evil: pride, and arrogancy, and the evil way, and the froward mouth, do I hate" (Proverbs 8:13). We must stand fast against it. Isaiah 5:18 says they "draw iniquity with cords of vanity." They "call evil good, and good evil." Isn't that what we see more and more in these days that we live in?

Woe unto them that *draw iniquity with cords of vanity, and sin as it were with a cart rope*: That say, Let him make speed, and hasten his work, that we may see it: and let the counsel of the Holy One of Israel draw nigh and come, that we may know it! *Woe unto them that call evil good, and good evil; that put darkness for light, and light for darkness; that put bitter for sweet, and sweet for bitter!* Woe unto them that are *wise in their own eyes, and prudent in their own sight!* Woe unto them that are *mighty to drink wine, and men of strength to mingle strong drink: Which justify the wicked for reward, and take away the righteousness of the righteous from him!* Therefore as the fire devoureth the stubble, and the flame consumeth the chaff, so their root shall be as rottenness, and their blossom shall go up as dust: because

they have cast away the law of the LORD of hosts,
and despised the word of the Holy One of Israel.
(Isaiah 5:18–24)

The wicked are "brute beasts" who take great pleasure in their sins, even to the point of mocking the Lord. However, we know that Galatians 6:7–8 says,

> Be not deceived; God is not mocked: for whatsoever a man soweth, that shall he also reap. For he that soweth to his flesh shall of the flesh reap corruption; but he that soweth to the Spirit shall of the Spirit reap life everlasting.

The Lord paid for our sins on Calvary—past, present, and future—*so should we continue in sin?* God forbid. It is our personal responsibility to not sin.

> Sanctify yourselves therefore, and be ye holy: for I am the Lord your God. (Leviticus 20:7)

> But as he which hath called you is holy, so be ye holy in all manner of conversation. (1 Peter 1:15)

> Because it is written, Be ye holy; for I am holy. (1 Peter 1:16)

> My little children, these things write I unto you, that ye sin not. And if any man sin, we have an advocate with the Father, Jesus Christ the righteous. (1 John 2:1)

A soldier for Christ must not be burdened with sin. As 1 John 1:9 says, "if we confess our sins, he is faithful and just to forgive us our sins, and to cleanse us from all unrighteousness."

What does the enemy want?

In the earthly realm, the enemy wants power, wealth, territory, and glory. In the spiritual realm, Satan wants souls, and he wants to be God. That is the original sin—man wanting to be God. We see it in the Garden of Eden when "the serpent said unto the woman, Ye shall not surely die: For God doth know that in the day ye eat thereof, then your eyes shall be opened, and *ye shall be as gods*, knowing good and evil" (Genesis 3:4–5). The devil lures us into his trap and then puts us in bondage, just like a spider weaves its web. Sadly, we are often tangled in our own web.

How does the enemy attack?

Satan lures his prey with deceit and temptations—trick or treat! He plays on our weaknesses. Genesis 4:7 warns us, "If thou doest well, shalt thou not be accepted? and if thou doest not well, sin lieth at the door. And unto thee shall be his desire, and thou shalt rule over him." Satan waits for an opportune time to attack—when we are doubtful, depressed, fearful, or anxious. He exploits those feelings with accusations that pull the spirit of man down. This is the oppression of the wicked. They surround their victim and close in for the kill, as seen in Psalm 17.

> Keep me as the apple of the eye, hide me under the shadow of thy wings, *From the wicked that oppress me, from my deadly enemies, who compass me about.* They are inclosed in their own fat: with their mouth they speak proudly. They have now compassed us in our steps: they have set their eyes bowing down to the earth; Like as a lion that is greedy of his prey, and as it were

a young lion lurking in secret places. Arise, O
LORD, disappoint him, cast him down: deliver
my soul from the wicked, which is thy sword.
(Psalm 17:8–13)

Our hope is in the Lord. When the enemy attacks, the Christian soldier stands strong. His lamp is full of oil, the Holy Spirit of God. He knows that his sins are forgiven because of the death, burial, and resurrection of Jesus Christ. He is covered in the righteousness of Christ. He trusts in Christ and Christ alone. He is unwavering and not tossed to and fro because his faith is in the Lord. As Proverbs 14:27 says, "the fear of the LORD is a fountain of life, to depart from the snares of death." In contrast, "the LORD is known by the judgment which he executeth: the wicked is snared in the work of his own hands. Higgaion. Selah" (Psalm 9:16).

7

HAVE FAITH IN GOD
KNOW THAT THE LORD HAS
ALREADY WON THE BATTLE

Summary

This chapter looks at the essential component of the battle plan—faith in God. Soldiers must believe that the mission is required, that the plan is the best strategy, and that their leader is fully committed to a successful mission. God's mission is the Great Commission. God's strategy is the one and only way, through Jesus Christ. As the captain of the army, Christ will bring His people safely into the kingdom of God.

How does a soldier overcome fear?

God calls His soldiers. The military recruits their soldiers. What might be the attitude of a person joining the military? For some, it may be an option of last resort; for others, a patriotic duty. In either case, mixed emotions would be expected. Very often, starting is the hardest part. Once the training begins and the team coalesces, there can be a sense of comfort in belonging to a worthy cause. However, reality hits when it is time to deploy, then there can be an overwhelming fear.

In the military, preparedness mitigates fear. A soldier is trained to be fully equipped for victory. They have their own strength and strength in numbers. They have all the weapons and ammunition that may be needed. They have strong, knowledgeable leaders whom they trust to give the right commands.

In the spiritual realm, preparedness mitigates fear as well. A soldier for Christ is fully equipped with the Word of God and the Holy Spirit for victory to glorify God. They have the full armor of God for offense and defense. They have complete faith and trust in their mighty warrior—God. Their faith overcomes their fear. What does Psalm 24:8 say? "Who is this King of glory? The LORD strong and mighty, the LORD mighty in battle," as also seen in Deuteronomy 20.

> When thou goest out to battle against thine enemies, and seest horses, and chariots, and a people more than thou, be not afraid of them: for the LORD thy God is with thee, which brought thee up out of the land of Egypt. And it shall be, when ye are come nigh unto the battle, that the priest shall approach and speak unto the people, And shall say unto them, Hear, O Israel, ye approach this day unto battle against your enemies: let not your hearts faint, fear not, and do not tremble, neither be ye terrified because of them; For the LORD your God is he that goeth with you, to fight for you against your enemies, to save you. (Deuteronomy 20:1–4)

When the enemy attacks, the Christian soldier has two choices—to flee in fear or to stand in faith. It is one or the other.

> There is no fear in love; but perfect love casteth out fear: because fear hath torment. He that feareth is not made perfect in love. (1 John 4:18)

> Though an host should encamp against me, my heart shall not fear: though war should rise against me, in this will I be confident. (Psalm 27:3)

The Christian soldier knows that "the angel of the Lord encampeth round about them that fear him, and delivereth them" (Psalm 34:7).

Fear is overcome when we read and study God's Word.

> Thy word is a lamp unto my feet, and a light unto my path. (Psalm 119:105)

> Therefore shall ye lay up these my words in your heart and in your soul, and bind them for a sign upon your hand, that they may be as frontlets between your eyes. (Deuteronomy 11:18)

The following scriptures are just a few examples of those that would be good to carry into battle:

> In God I will praise his word, in God I have put my trust; I will not fear what flesh can do unto me. (Psalm 56)

> The Lord is on my side; I will not fear: what can man do unto me? (Psalm 118:6)

> Hearken unto me, ye that know righteousness, the people in whose heart is my law; fear ye not the reproach of men, neither be ye afraid of their revilings. (Isaiah 51:7)

> In the fear of the Lord is strong confidence: and his children shall have a place of refuge. (Proverbs 14:26)

Fear thou not; for I am with thee: be not dismayed; for I am thy God: I will strengthen thee; yea, I will help thee; yea, I will uphold thee with the right hand of my righteousness. (Isaiah 41:10)

No weapon that is formed against thee shall prosper; and every tongue that shall rise against thee in judgment thou shalt condemn. This is the heritage of the servants of the LORD, and their righteousness is of me, saith the LORD. (Isaiah 54:17)

He will keep the feet of his saints, and the wicked shall be silent in darkness; for by strength shall no man prevail. (1 Samuel 2:9)

The horse is prepared against the day of battle: but safety is of the LORD. (Proverbs 21:31)

For thou hast girded me with strength unto the battle: thou hast subdued under me those that rose up against me. (Psalm 18:39)

O God the Lord, the strength of my salvation, thou hast covered my head in the day of battle. (Psalm 140:7)

He hath delivered my soul in peace from the battle that was against me: for there were many with me. (Psalm 55:18)

Cast thy burden upon the LORD, and he shall sustain thee: he shall never suffer the righteous to be moved. (Psalm 55:22)

Most importantly, the Christian soldier must listen to the words of Jesus in Mark 11:22, "And Jesus answering saith unto them, Have faith in God." The Lord says to build up your Holy faith, and we know that "faith comes by hearing and hearing by the Word of God" (Romans 10:17). Through faith, mighty men of God fulfilled the will of God for the glory of God, as summarized in Hebrews 11. The Christian soldier follows in their footsteps, which most assuredly are the footsteps of Christ. *Through faith in Him, we pray with confidence rather than desperation.* We are not dismayed, "for God hath not given us the spirit of fear; but of power, and of love, and of a sound mind" (2 Timothy 1:7).

"Finally, my brethren, be strong in the Lord, and in the power of his might" (Ephesians 6:10), just like Gideon, the mighty man of valor in Judges 6,

> And there came an angel of the LORD, and sat under an oak which was in Ophrah, that pertained unto Joash the Abiezrite: and his son Gideon threshed wheat by the winepress, to hide it from the Midianites. And the angel of the LORD appeared unto him, and said unto him, The LORD is with thee, thou mighty man of valour. And Gideon said unto him, Oh my Lord, if the LORD be with us, why then is all this befallen us? and where be all his miracles which our fathers told us of, saying, Did not the LORD bring us up from Egypt? but now the LORD hath forsaken us, and delivered us into the hands of the Midianites. And the LORD looked upon him, and said, Go in this thy might, and thou shalt save Israel from the hand of the Midianites: *have not I sent thee?* And he said unto him, Oh my Lord, wherewith shall I save Israel? behold, my family is poor in Manasseh, and I am the least in my father's house. And the LORD said unto him,

> Surely I will be with thee, and thou shalt smite
> the Midianites as one man. (Judges 6:11–16)

The Lord led Gideon through a series of events so that he would trust Him in the battle. Gideon came to understand that he went in the name of the Lord and in the name of Gideon! Gideon declares this in Judges 7:18: "When I blow with a trumpet, I and all that are with me, then blow ye the trumpets also on every side of all the camp, and say, The sword of the LORD, and of Gideon." The true Christian soldier, with full faith in the Lord, can truly say, "I go in the name of the Lord and in the name of ___________ [fill in your own name]!"

Gideon asked for a sign from the Lord for assurance of the call to battle. And they asked Jesus for a sign as well, but He said in Matthew 12:39, "There shall no sign be given to it, but the sign of the prophet Jonas." When God calls His soldiers, there is only one answer: "Here am I; send me" (Isaiah 6:8). The Lord is our refuge and fortress in the battle as we read in Psalm 91.

> He that dwelleth in the secret place of the
> most High shall abide under the shadow of the
> Almighty. I will say of the LORD, He is my ref-
> uge and my fortress: my God; in him will I trust.
> Surely he shall deliver thee from the snare of the
> fowler, and from the noisome pestilence. He shall
> cover thee with his feathers, and under his wings
> shalt thou trust: his truth shall be thy shield and
> buckler. Thou shalt not be afraid for the terror
> by night; nor for the arrow that flieth by day;
> Nor for the pestilence that walketh in darkness;
> nor for the destruction that wasteth at noonday.
> A thousand shall fall at thy side, and ten thou-
> sand at thy right hand; but it shall not come nigh
> thee. Only with thine eyes shalt thou behold and
> see the reward of the wicked. Because thou hast
> made the LORD, which is my refuge, even the

most High, thy habitation; There shall no evil befall thee, neither shall any plague come nigh thy dwelling. For he shall give his angels charge over thee, to keep thee in all thy ways. They shall bear thee up in their hands, lest thou dash thy foot against a stone. Thou shalt tread upon the lion and adder: the young lion and the dragon shalt thou trample under feet. Because he hath set his love upon me, therefore will I deliver him: I will set him on high, because he hath known my name. He shall call upon me, and I will answer him: I will be with him in trouble; I will deliver him, and honour him. With long life will I satisfy him, and shew him my salvation. (Psalm 91)

When the world presses in, there are really only two choices—fight the Lord or trust the Lord. *When we are cornered and there is no way out, what do we do?* There is the way of life and the way of death. There is no other way. Remember how the disciples of Christ answered this question in John 6:68: "Simon Peter answered him, Lord, to whom shall we go? thou hast the words of eternal life."

Yes, the Lord does the work of salvation, and we cannot lose our salvation. However, it is a two-way relationship that requires faith, love, and wisdom. It is our personal responsibility to pray, to ask, and to seek the will of our Father through Jesus Christ. As Deuteronomy 30:19 says,

> I call heaven and earth to record this day against you, that I have set before you life and death, blessing and cursing: therefore choose life, that both thou and thy seed may live.

Jesus said it very clearly: "I am the way, the truth, and the life: no man cometh unto the Father, but by me" (John 14:6).

In Psalm 11, King David expresses his faith in the Lord in the midst of the battle.

> In the LORD put I my trust: how say ye to my soul, Flee as a bird to your mountain? For, lo, the wicked bend their bow, they make ready their arrow upon the string, that they may privily shoot at the upright in heart. If the foundations be destroyed, what can the righteous do? The LORD is in his holy temple, the LORD's throne is in heaven: his eyes behold, his eyelids try, the children of men. The LORD trieth the righteous: but the wicked and him that loveth violence his soul hateth. Upon the wicked he shall rain snares, fire and brimstone, and an horrible tempest: this shall be the portion of their cup. For the righteous LORD loveth righteousness; his countenance doth behold the upright. (Psalm 11)

We are not to be afraid because the Lord is with us. Deuteronomy 31:6 says,

> Be strong and of a good courage, fear not, nor be afraid of them: for the LORD thy God, he it is that doth go with thee; he will not fail thee, nor forsake thee.

We should "be not afraid of sudden fear, neither of the desolation of the wicked, when it cometh" (Proverbs 3:25). "For thou hast girded me with strength unto the battle: thou hast subdued under me those that rose up against me" (Psalm 18:39).

The book of Jude clearly lays out the battle ground and the faith that is required to have the victory through our Lord Jesus Christ.

> Jude, the servant of Jesus Christ, and brother of James, to them that are *sanctified* by

God the Father, and *preserved* in Jesus Christ, and called: Mercy unto you, and peace, and love, be multiplied. Beloved, when I gave all diligence to write unto you of the common salvation, it was needful for me to write unto you, and exhort you that ye should *earnestly contend for the faith* which was once delivered unto the saints. For there are certain men crept in unawares, who were before of old ordained to this condemnation, ungodly men, turning the grace of our God into lasciviousness, and denying the only Lord God, and our Lord Jesus Christ. I will therefore put you in remembrance, though ye once knew this, how that the Lord, having saved the people out of the land of Egypt, afterward destroyed them that believed not. And the angels which kept not their first estate, but left their own habitation, he hath reserved in everlasting chains under darkness unto the judgment of the great day. Even as Sodom and Gomorrha, and the cities about them in like manner, giving themselves over to fornication, and going after strange flesh, are set forth for an example, suffering the vengeance of eternal fire. Likewise also these filthy dreamers defile the flesh, despise dominion, and speak evil of dignities. Yet Michael the archangel, when contending with the devil he disputed about the body of Moses, durst not bring against him a railing accusation, but said, The Lord rebuke thee. But these speak evil of those things which they know not: but what they know naturally, as brute beasts, in those things they corrupt themselves. Woe unto them! for they have gone in the way of Cain, and ran greedily after the error of Balaam for reward, and perished in the gainsaying of Core. (Jude 1–11)

These are spots in your feasts of charity, when they feast with you, feeding themselves without fear: clouds they are without water, carried about of winds; trees whose fruit withereth, without fruit, twice dead, plucked up by the roots; Raging waves of the sea, foaming out their own shame; wandering stars, to whom is reserved the blackness of darkness for ever. And Enoch also, the seventh from Adam, prophesied of these, saying, Behold, the Lord cometh with ten thousands of his saints, To execute judgment upon all, and to convince all that are ungodly among them of all their ungodly deeds which they have ungodly committed, and of all their hard speeches which ungodly sinners have spoken against him. These are murmurers, complainers, walking after their own lusts; and their mouth speaketh great swelling words, having men's persons in admiration because of advantage. But, beloved, remember ye the words which were spoken before of the apostles of our Lord Jesus Christ; How that they told you there should be mockers in the last time, who should walk after their own ungodly lusts. These be they who separate themselves, sensual, having not the Spirit. But ye, beloved, building up yourselves on your most holy faith, praying in the Holy Ghost, Keep yourselves in the love of God, looking for the mercy of our Lord Jesus Christ unto eternal life. And of some have compassion, making a difference: And others save with fear, pulling them out of the fire; hating even the garment spotted by the flesh. Now unto him that is able to keep you from falling, and to present you faultless before the presence of his glory with exceeding joy, To the only wise God our Saviour,

be glory and majesty, dominion and power, both
now and ever. Amen. (Jude 12–25)

We are sanctified, preserved, and called (verse 1). The Lord calls
out His warriors to earnestly contend for the faith (verse 3). Why?
"There are certain men crept in unawares, who were before of old
ordained to this condemnation" (verse 4). The battle has been raging
from the beginning—"ungodly men, turning the grace of our God
into lasciviousness, and denying the only Lord God, and our Lord
Jesus Christ" (verse 4).

The following verses are to remind us of God's victory:

Having saved the people out of the land of
Egypt, afterward destroyed them that believed
not. (verse 5)

[The angels] reserved in everlasting chains
under darkness. (verse 6)

And, the saving of Lot's family before the
annihilation of Sodom and Gomorrah. (verse 7)

The book of Jude condemns them who have "gone the way of
Cain," who are like "raging waves of the sea, foaming out their own
shame; wandering stars, to whom is reserved the blackness of darkness for ever" (verse 13). This is the enemy, but "ye are of God, little
children, and have overcome them: because greater is he that is in
you, than he that is in the world" (1 John 4:4). In the end, we will be
coming with Christ! "Behold, the Lord cometh with ten thousands
of his saints" (verse 14).

*The bottom line is this: Jesus is inside of us, and we are inside of
Him. This is our confidence. This is the strength of our faith in God:
"Christ in you the hope of glory"* (Colossians 1:27).

8

PUT ON THE WHOLE ARMOR OF GOD GET IN THE FIGHT

Summary

Chapter 8 equips the Christian soldier for battle. Ephesians 6:11 says to "put on the whole armour of God, that ye may be able to stand against the wiles of the devil." And we know that "all scripture is given by inspiration of God, and is profitable for doctrine, for reproof, for correction, for instruction in righteousness: That the man of God may be perfect, throughly furnished unto all good works" (2 Timothy 3:18–19). We can be fully equipped for the battle through the Word of God!

The soldier's creed

A good soldier must know when to fight, retreat, or stand down using both offensive and defensive strategies. The military uses the term "situational awareness." The Bible uses the word *circumspect*—"that ye walk circumspectly, not as fools, but as wise, redeeming the time, because the days are evil" (Ephesians 5:15–16). If we have the wisdom of God, we will not be caught off guard (as a thief in the night) but remain on guard against the wiles of the devil.

The army's Soldier's Creed is a good motto for a Christian soldier to follow:

- I am an American Soldier.
- I am a warrior and a member of a team.
- I serve the people of the United States and live the army values.
- I will always place the mission first.
- I will never accept defeat.
- I will never quit.
- I will never leave a fallen comrade.
- I am disciplined, physically and mentally tough, trained and proficient in my warrior tasks and drills.
- I always maintain my arms, my equipment, and myself.
- I am an expert, and I am a professional.
- I stand ready to deploy, engage, and destroy the enemies of the United States of America in close combat.
- I am a guardian of freedom and the American way of life.
- I am an American soldier.

As a Christian soldier:

- I am a Christian soldier.
- I am a warrior and a member of a team.
- I serve God and His people and live the Lord's values.
- I will always place God's Great Commission first.
- I will never accept defeat.
- I will never quit.
- I will never leave a fallen comrade.
- I am disciplined, physically and mentally tough, trained and proficient in my warrior tasks and drills.
- I always maintain my arms, my equipment, and myself.
- I am an expert, and I am a professional.
- I remain ready to deploy, engage, and stand against the enemies of the Lord.
- I am a guardian of freedom and the Lord's way of life.
- I am a Christian soldier.

The whole armor of God

As the soldier says, "I maintain my arms, my equipment and myself," so the Christian maintains the whole armor of God. This is personal responsibility, as shown in Ephesians 6:10–18.

> Finally, my brethren, be strong in the Lord, and in the power of his might. Put on the whole armour of God, that ye may be able to stand against the wiles of the devil. For we wrestle not against flesh and blood, but against principalities, against powers, against the rulers of the darkness of this world, against spiritual wickedness in high places. Wherefore take unto you the whole armour of God, that ye may be able to withstand in the evil day, and having done all, to stand. Stand therefore, having your *loins girt about with truth*, and having on the *breastplate of righteousness; And your feet shod with the preparation of the gospel of peace*; Above all, taking the *shield of faith*, wherewith ye shall be able to quench all the fiery darts of the wicked. And take the *helmet of salvation*, and the *sword of the Spirit, which is the word of God*: Praying always with all prayer and supplication in the Spirit, and watching thereunto with all perseverance and supplication for all saints. (Ephesians 6:10–18)

The active verbs in these verses are *wrestle* and *stand*. There is a time to fight and a time to cease from fighting, "a time of war and a time of peace" (Ecclesiastes 3:8). In either case, the preparations for battle are very important. As Joel 3:9 says, "Proclaim ye this among the Gentiles; Prepare war, wake up the mighty men, let all the men of war draw near; let them come up." We prepare by putting on *every piece* of the armor of God.

What does it mean to have your loins girt about with truth? One who is grounded in the Word of God will not be tossed to and fro and not shaken when the enemy attacks. This knowledge is an essential defensive tool against the deceit and lies of the wicked. As Hosea 4:6 says, "My people are destroyed for lack of knowledge." The Christian soldier seeks knowledge, as Proverbs 18:15 says, "The heart of the prudent getteth knowledge; and the ear of the wise seeketh knowledge."

What is the breastplate of righteousness? The breastplate of righteousness is the righteousness of Jesus Christ, which is imputed unto His children in salvation. "And if Christ be in you, the body is dead because of sin; but the Spirit is life because of righteousness" (Romans 8:10). This is the Lord's work. Our personal responsibility is to be renewed in the Spirit daily "and that ye put on the new man, which after God is created in righteousness and true holiness" (Ephesians 4:24). As Job said in Job 29:14, "I put on righteousness, and it clothed me: my judgment was as a robe and a diadem." It is the Lord's righteousness, as Psalm 119:142 declares, "Thy righteousness is an everlasting righteousness, and thy law is the truth." God's children should seek Him with their whole heart, for "blessed are they which do hunger and thirst after righteousness: for they shall be filled" (Matthew 5:6).

The Lord said it clearly through the prophet Hosea: "Sow to yourselves in righteousness, reap in mercy; break up your fallow ground: for it is time to seek the LORD, till he come and rain righteousness upon you" (Hosea 10:12). The Old Testament saints fought and won many battles when they went in the name of the Lord. They learned that it was futile to fight in their own strength. It is His righteousness and His alone. Therein is the contrast between the Law and grace, as seen in Philippians 3:9: "And be found in him, not having mine own righteousness, which is of the law, but that which is through the faith of Christ, the righteousness which is of God by faith." The Lord's righteousness echoes throughout the Bible. Here are just a few verses:

> Little children, let no man deceive you: he
> that doeth righteousness is righteous, even as he
> is righteous. (1 John 3:7)

Being filled with the fruits of righteousness, which are by Jesus Christ, unto the glory and praise of God. (Philippians 1:11)

He that followeth after righteousness and mercy findeth life, righteousness, and honour. (Proverbs 21:21)

Let thy priests be clothed with righteousness; and let thy saints shout for joy. (Psalm 132:9)

Lead me, O LORD, in thy righteousness because of mine enemies; make thy way straight before my face. (Psalm 5:8)

Righteousness keepeth him that is upright in the way: but wickedness overthroweth the sinner. (Proverbs 13:6)

Hearken unto me, ye that know righteousness, the people in whose heart is my law; fear ye not the reproach of men, neither be ye afraid of their revilings. (Isaiah 51:7)

But and if ye suffer for righteousness' sake, happy are ye: and be not afraid of their terror, neither be troubled. (1 Peter 3:14)

Blessed are they which are persecuted for righteousness' sake: for theirs is the kingdom of heaven. (Matthew 5:10)

Soldiers put on the uniform of the military branch they serve. This is required. It displays the unity, compliance, and obedience of the force. The Christian soldier is covered with the righteousness of Christ. This is the white robe of Christ's righteousness that covers His chosen people. Those who do not have on the proper garments are cast out, as seen in Matthew 22:11–14. "Their webs shall not become garments, neither shall they cover themselves with their works: their works are works of iniquity, and the act of violence is in their hands" (Isaiah 59:6).

> And when the king came in to see the guests, he saw there a man which had not on a wedding garment: And he saith unto him, Friend, how camest thou in hither not having a wedding garment? And he was speechless. Then said the king to the servants, Bind him hand and foot, and take him away, and cast him into outer darkness; there shall be weeping and gnashing of teeth. *For many are called, but few are chosen.* (Matthew 22:11–14)

What does it mean to have your feet shod with the preparation of the gospel of peace? The military leaders believe in "peace through strength." The Christian soldier believes in peace through Christ. "I can do all things through Christ which strengtheneth me" (Philippians 4:13).

This soldier walks in the footsteps of Jesus with the peace that passes all understanding.

> A soft answer turneth away wrath: but grievous words stir up anger. (Proverbs 15:1)

> And the fruit of righteousness is sown in peace of them that make peace. (James 3:18)

As God's soldiers go into the battlefield, they go in peace, seeking those who may be saved. "And if the house be worthy, let your peace come upon it: but if it be not worthy, let your peace return to you" (Matthew 10:13). We are to shake off the dust and carry on for the cause of Christ.

What is the shield of faith, wherewith ye shall be able to quench all the fiery darts of the wicked? Wise soldiers learn how to protect themselves from those who attack. They practice various maneuvers to defend themselves from harm. A wounded soldier is hindered in his ability to fight. The devil's "fiery darts" can knock a person down emotionally, physically, and spiritually. The shield of faith counteracts those attacks with assurance in the promises of God. This is the confidence that we have in the Lord.

> For the LORD shall be thy confidence, and shall keep thy foot from being taken. (Proverbs 3:26)

> For thus saith the Lord God, the Holy One of Israel; In returning and rest shall ye be saved; in quietness and in confidence shall be your strength: and ye would not. (Isaiah 30:15)

How many times have we gone into a battle without the Lord? It is not wise to go without being fully equipped. The Psalms repeatedly tell of the importance of the shield of faith.

> Thou art my hiding place and my shield: I hope in thy word. (Psalm 119:114)

> Behold, O God our shield, and look upon the face of thine anointed. (Psalm 84:9)

> But thou, O LORD, art a shield for me; my glory, and the lifter up of mine head. (Psalm 3:3)

> Every word of God is pure: he is a shield unto them that put their trust in him. (Proverbs 30:5)

Our soul waiteth for the LORD: he is our help and our shield. (Psalm 33:20)

My goodness, and my fortress; my high tower, and my deliverer; my shield, and he in whom I trust; who subdueth my people under me. (Psalm 144:2)

David, a man after God's own heart, says it best in 2 Samuel 22:

And David spake unto the LORD the words of this song in the day that the LORD had delivered him out of the hand of all his enemies, and out of the hand of Saul: And he said, The LORD is my rock, and my fortress, and my deliverer; The God of my rock; in him will I trust: he is my shield, and the horn of my salvation, my high tower, and my refuge, my saviour; thou savest me from violence. I will call on the LORD, who is worthy to be praised: so shall I be saved from mine enemies. When the waves of death compassed me, the floods of ungodly men made me afraid; The sorrows of hell compassed me about; the snares of death prevented me; In my distress I called upon the LORD, and cried to my God: and he did hear my voice out of his temple, and my cry did enter into his ears. Then the earth shook and trembled; the foundations of heaven moved and shook, because he was wroth. There went up a smoke out of his nostrils, and fire out of his mouth devoured: coals were kindled by it. He bowed the heavens also, and came down; and darkness was under his feet. And he rode upon a cherub, and did fly: and he was seen upon the wings of the wind. And he made darkness pavilions round about him, dark waters, and thick clouds of the skies. Through the brightness before him were coals of fire kindled. The LORD thundered from heaven, and the most High uttered his voice. And he sent out arrows, and scattered them; lightning, and discomfited them. (2 Samuel 22:1–15)

And the channels of the sea appeared, the foundations of the world were discovered, at the rebuking of the LORD, at the blast of the breath of his nostrils. He sent from above, he took me; he drew me out of many waters; He delivered me from my strong enemy, and from them that hated me: for they were too strong for me. They prevented me in the day of my calamity: but the LORD was my stay. He brought me forth also into a large place: he delivered me, because he delighted in me. The LORD rewarded me according to my righteousness: according to the cleanness of my hands hath he recompensed me. For I have kept the ways of the LORD, and have not wickedly departed from my God. For all his judgments were before me: and as for his statutes, I did not depart from them. I was also upright before him, and have kept myself from mine iniquity. Therefore the LORD hath recompensed me according to my righteousness; according to my cleanness in his eye sight. With the merciful thou wilt shew thyself merciful, and with the upright man thou wilt shew thyself upright. With the pure thou wilt shew thyself pure; and with the froward thou wilt shew thyself unsavoury. And the afflicted people thou wilt save: but thine eyes are upon the haughty, that thou mayest bring them down. For thou art my lamp, O LORD: and the LORD will lighten my darkness. For by thee

I have run through a troop: by my God have I leaped over a wall. (2 Samuel 22:16–30)

As for God, his way is perfect; the word of the LORD is tried: he is a buckler to all them that trust in him. For who is God, save the LORD? and who is a rock, save our God? God is my strength and power: and he maketh my way perfect. He maketh my feet like hinds' feet: and setteth me upon my high places. He teacheth my hands to war; so that a bow of steel is broken by mine arms. Thou hast also given me the shield of thy salvation: and thy gentleness hath made me great. Thou hast enlarged my steps under me; so that my feet did not slip. I have pursued mine enemies, and destroyed them; and turned not again until I had consumed them. And I have consumed them, and wounded them, that they could not arise: yea, they are fallen under my feet. For thou hast girded me with strength to battle: them that rose up against me hast thou subdued under me. Thou hast also given me the necks of mine enemies, that I might destroy them that hate me. They looked, but there was none to save; even unto the LORD, but he answered them not. Then did I beat them as small as the dust of the earth, I did stamp them as the mire of the street, and did spread them abroad. Thou also hast delivered me from the strivings of my people, thou hast kept me to be head of the heathen: a people which I knew not shall serve me. Strangers shall submit themselves unto me: as soon as they hear, they shall be obedient unto me. Strangers shall fade away, and they shall be afraid out of their close places. The Lord liveth; and blessed be my rock; and exalted be the God of the rock of my salvation. It is God that avengeth me, and that bringeth down the people under me, And that bringeth me forth from mine enemies: thou also hast lifted me up on high above them that rose up against me: thou hast delivered me from the violent man. Therefore I will give thanks unto thee, O Lord, among the heathen, and I will sing praises unto thy name. He is the tower of salvation for his king: and sheweth mercy to his anointed, unto David, and to his seed for ever-more. (2 Samuel 22:31–51)

What is the helmet of salvation? The Lord opens our heart, fills us with His Holy Spirit, and gives us direct access to the mind of Christ. "For who hath known the mind of the Lord, that he may instruct him? But we have the mind of Christ" (1 Corinthians 2:16). He secures us for all eternity. However, our personal responsibility is to seek out the mind of Christ and protect ourselves from the forces that want to bring confusion and doubt. Our mind can rest in the "simplicity of Christ." For God is not the author of confusion.

"Jesus said unto him, Thou shalt love the Lord thy God with all thy heart, and with all thy soul, and with all thy mind" (Matthew 22:37). Our mind determines our actions. "I thank God through Jesus Christ our Lord. So then with the mind I myself serve the law of God; but with the flesh the law of sin" (Romans 7:25). We must put on the helmet to guard our thoughts against the lusts of the flesh. "But let us, who are of the day, be sober, putting on the breast-plate of faith and love; and for an helmet, the hope of salvation" (1 Thessalonians 5:8).

With the mind of Christ, the Christian soldier will be ready for the day of vengeance that is to come upon the earth. We put on the whole armor of God with Jesus as our example and commander in chief. "For he put on righteousness as a breastplate, and an helmet of salvation upon his head; and he put on the garments of vengeance for clothing, and was clad with zeal as a cloke" (Isaiah 59:17). It is good to read this in context, as seen in Isaiah 59:7–21.

> Their feet run to evil, and they make haste to shed innocent blood: their thoughts are thoughts of iniquity; wasting and destruction are in their paths. The way of peace they know not; and there is no judgment in their goings: they have made them crooked paths: whosoever goeth therein shall not know peace. Therefore is judgment far from us, neither doth justice overtake us: we wait for light, but behold obscurity; for brightness, but we walk in darkness. We grope for the wall like the blind, and we grope as if we had no eyes: we stumble at noonday as in the night; we are in desolate places as dead men. We roar all like bears, and mourn sore like doves: we look for judgment, but there is none; for salvation, but it is far off from us. For our transgressions are multiplied before thee, and our sins testify against us: for our transgressions are with us; and as for our iniquities, we know them; In transgressing and lying against the LORD, and departing away from our God, speaking oppression and revolt, conceiving and uttering from the heart words of falsehood. (Isaiah 59:7–13)

> And judgment is turned away backward, and justice standeth afar off: for truth is fallen in the street, and equity cannot enter. Yea, truth faileth; and he that departeth from evil maketh himself a prey: and the LORD saw it, and it displeased him that there was no judgment. And he saw that there was no man, and wondered that there was no intercessor: therefore his arm brought salvation unto him; and his righteous-

ness, it sustained him. *For he put on righteousness as a breastplate, and an helmet of salvation upon his head; and he put on the garments of vengeance for clothing, and was clad with zeal as a cloke.* According to their deeds, accordingly he will repay, fury to his adversaries, recompence to his enemies; to the islands he will repay recompence. So shall they fear the name of the Lord from the west, and his glory from the rising of the sun. When the enemy shall come in like a flood, the Spirit of the Lord shall lift up a standard against him. And the Redeemer shall come to Zion, and unto them that turn from transgression in Jacob, saith the Lord. As for me, this is my covenant with them, saith the Lord; My spirit that is upon thee, and my words which I have put in thy mouth, shall not depart out of thy mouth, nor out of the mouth of thy seed, nor out of the mouth of thy seed's seed, saith the Lord, from henceforth and for ever. (Isaiah 59:14–21)

What is the sword of the Spirit? The sword is a weapon of offense and defense. For the Christian soldier, it is the Word of God, which cuts both ways. It cuts some into the kingdom of God and cuts some out, and it will not return void.

So shall my word be that goeth forth out of my mouth: it shall not return unto me void, but it shall accomplish that which I please, and it shall prosper in the thing whereto I sent it. (Isaiah 55:11)

The sword is to be used for the Lord's holy purpose, as Matthew 10:34 says, "Think not that I am come to send peace on earth: I came not to send peace, but a sword."

This sword of the Lord is infinitely powerful. Only those who are worthy are given the right to use it. We are not worthy. It is Christ in us who is worthy. However, we must strive to fulfill this high calling, as the Lord says in 1 Thessalonians 2:12, "That ye would walk worthy of God, who hath called you unto his kingdom and glory." It is a great honor to be able to wield this sword.

> For the word of God is quick, and powerful, and sharper than any two edged sword, piercing even to the dividing asunder of soul and spirit, and of the joints and marrow, and is a discerner of the thoughts and intents of the heart. (Hebrews 4:12)

With this powerful sword comes great responsibility. It is not only to be used aggressively but also gently. The Christian soldier does not want to be overbearing. The wisdom of God is required.

There is an interesting parallel with fishing. A good fisherman knows how to wait even when the line begins to be pulled. If you try to hook the fish too soon, it may be spooked and let go of the bait. The time to hook is when the fish is really running with it. Christ calls us to be "fishers of men," and that requires a sincere perception of those you are trying to reach. If you come on too strong, they may run away. The Word of God is often taken a little at a time. "Precept upon precept," as the Lord says in Isaiah 28.

How do we win the victory? The Christian soldier maintains the armor of God, knows the enemy, discerns the spirits, boldly shares the gospel, and resists the devil. He does not let his guard down. Through faith, perseverance, and resilience, he stands against the wiles of the devil. As James 4:7 says, "Submit yourselves therefore to God. Resist the devil, and he will flee from you."

The training ground is the visible local church founded by the authority of Jesus Christ. Here is where we worship the Lord, pray together, learn His Word, and fellowship. Here is where we build each other up in the holy faith. Iron sharpens iron. As Proverbs 27:17 says, "Iron sharpeneth iron; so a man sharpeneth the countenance of his friend." We are workers together with Christ, as seen in 2 Corinthians 6.

> We then, as workers together with him, beseech you also that ye receive not the grace of God in vain. (For he saith, I have heard thee in a time accepted, and in the day of salvation have I succoured thee: behold, now is the accepted time; behold, now is the day of salvation.) Giving no offence in any thing, that the ministry be not blamed: But in all things approving ourselves as the ministers of God, in much patience, in afflictions, in necessities, in distresses, In stripes, in imprisonments, in tumults, in labours, in watchings, in fastings; By pureness, by knowledge, by longsuffering, by kindness, by the Holy Ghost, by love unfeigned, By the word of truth, by the power of God, by the armour of righteousness on the right hand and on the left, By honour and dishonour, by evil report and good report: as deceivers, and yet true; As unknown, and yet well known; as dying, and, behold, we live; as chastened, and not killed; As sorrowful, yet alway rejoicing; as poor, yet making many rich; as having nothing, and yet possessing all things. (2 Corinthians 6:1–10)

The victory is in the fulfillment of God's purpose for your life. *Only what is done for Christ lasts.* We want to hear those precious words, "His lord said unto him, Well done, good and faithful servant; thou hast been faithful over a few things, I will make thee ruler over many things: enter thou into the joy of thy lord" (Matthew 25:23).

9

WAIT ON THE LORD
BE STILL AND KNOW THAT
GOD IS IN CONTROL

Summary

Chapter 9 analyzes what could be one of the most difficult military assignments—learning how to wait. Here you are on fire for God, fully committed, trained, and equipped for the battle, like a racehorse waiting for the gate to open, and the Lord says wait. This can cause frustration, anxiety, doubt, and even depression.

When you don't feel like you're being used by God

One may question, "Why is the Lord not using me?" At this point, it is good to remember the example of the yoke that Jesus describes in Matthew 11:28–30.

> Come unto me, all ye that labour and are
> heavy laden, and I will give you rest. Take my
> yoke upon you, and learn of me; for I am meek
> and lowly in heart: and ye shall find rest unto
> your souls. For my yoke is easy, and my burden
> is light.

The wooden yoke has two neck collars. Jesus is in one, and His child is in the other. If the child pushes forward ahead of the Lord, there is strain and stress. If the child lags behind, he may cry, "Woe is me! I can't make it any further." However, if the child walks alongside of the Lord, He carries all the weight in His perfect timing! "To every thing there is a season, and a time to every purpose under the heaven" (Ecclesiastes 3:1).

There may be times when we do not even need to fight in the battle. We see this in 2 Chronicles, where "the children of Moab, and the children of Ammon, and with them other beside the Ammonites, came against Jehoshaphat to battle."

> And Judah gathered themselves together, to ask help of the LORD: even out of all the cities of Judah they came to seek the LORD. And Jehoshaphat stood in the congregation of Judah and Jerusalem, in the house of the LORD, before the new court, And said, O LORD God of our fathers, art not thou God in heaven? and rulest not thou over all the kingdoms of the heathen? and in thine hand is there not power and might, so that none is able to withstand thee? Art not thou our God, who didst drive out the inhabitants of this land before thy people Israel, and gavest it to the seed of Abraham thy friend for ever? And they dwelt therein, and have built thee a sanctuary therein for thy name, saying, If, when evil cometh upon us, as the sword, judgment, or pestilence, or famine, we stand before this house, and in thy presence, (for thy name is in this house,) and cry unto thee in our affliction, then thou wilt hear and help. (2 Chronicles 20:4–9)

> And all Judah stood before the LORD, with their little ones, their wives, and their children. Then upon Jahaziel the son of Zechariah, the son

of Benaiah, the son of Jeiel, the son of Mattaniah, a Levite of the sons of Asaph, came the Spirit of the LORD in the midst of the congregation; And he said, Hearken ye, all Judah, and ye inhabitants of Jerusalem, and thou king Jehoshaphat, Thus saith the LORD unto you, *Be not afraid nor dismayed by reason of this great multitude; for the battle is not yours, but God's.* To morrow go ye down against them: behold, they come up by the cliff of Ziz; and ye shall find them at the end of the brook, before the wilderness of Jeruel. *Ye shall not need to fight in this battle*: set yourselves, stand ye still, and see the salvation of the LORD with you, O Judah and Jerusalem: fear not, nor be dismayed; to morrow go out against them: for the LORD will be with you. (2 Chronicles 20:13–17)

God's power, not ours

The important thing to remember is that we have no power on our own. As Ephesians 1:19 says, it is His power to us. "And what is the exceeding greatness of his power to us-ward who believe, according to the working of his mighty power." It is futile to go into the battle on our own power. The Lord goes before us to prepare the hearts and to position the enemy. Everything is orchestrated according to His holy plan. The Lord will stop us if it is not in His timing. "The preparations of the heart in man, and the answer of the tongue, is from the LORD" (Proverbs 16:1).

The Lord says, "Be still, and know that I am God: I will be exalted among the heathen, I will be exalted in the earth" (Psalm 46:10). A good soldier must know how to wait on the Lord, but waiting does not mean doing nothing. It is a time of continued prayer and preparation.

Watch ye, stand fast in the faith, quit you like men, be strong. (1 Corinthians 16:13)

Take ye heed, watch and pray: for ye know
not when the time is. (Mark 13:33)

We do not want to be caught by surprise, as the thief in the
night in 1 Thessalonians.

But of the times and the seasons, brethren,
ye have no need that I write unto you. For yourselves know perfectly that the day of the Lord
so cometh as a thief in the night. *For when they
shall say, Peace and safety; then sudden destruction
cometh upon them*, as travail upon a woman with
child; and they shall not escape. But ye, brethren,
are not in darkness, that that day should overtake
you as a thief. Ye are all the children of light, and
the children of the day: we are not of the night,
nor of darkness. *Therefore let us not sleep, as do
others; but let us watch and be sober.* For they that
sleep sleep in the night; and they that be drunken
are drunken in the night. But let us, who are of
the day, be sober, *putting on the breastplate of faith
and love; and for an helmet, the hope of salvation.
For God hath not appointed us to wrath*, but to
obtain salvation by our Lord Jesus Christ, Who
died for us, that, whether we wake or sleep, we
should live together with him. *Wherefore comfort
yourselves together, and edify one another, even as
also ye do.* (1 Thessalonians 5:1–11)

And we beseech you, brethren, to know
them which labour among you, and are over you
in the Lord, and admonish you; And to esteem
them very highly in love for their work's sake.
And be at peace among yourselves. Now we
exhort you, brethren, warn them that are unruly,
comfort the feebleminded, support the weak,

be patient toward all men. See that none render evil for evil unto any man; but ever follow that which is good, both among yourselves, and to all men. Rejoice evermore. Pray without ceasing. In every thing give thanks: for this is the will of God in Christ Jesus concerning you. Quench not the Spirit. Despise not prophesyings. Prove all things; hold fast that which is good. Abstain from all appearance of evil. And the very God of peace sanctify you wholly; and I pray God your whole spirit and soul and body be preserved blameless unto the coming of our Lord Jesus Christ. Faithful is he that calleth you, who also will do it. Brethren, pray for us. Greet all the brethren with an holy kiss. I charge you by the Lord that this epistle be read unto all the holy brethren. The grace of our Lord Jesus Christ be with you. Amen. (1 Thessalonians 5:12–28)

Note: the first epistle to the Thessalonians was written from Athens. As we wait upon the Lord, there can be great peace, knowing that the wrath of God will never come upon the saints. As 1 Thessalonians 5:9 says, "God hath not appointed us to wrath." This is confirmed in Romans 5:9, which says, "Much more then, being now justified by his blood, we shall be saved from wrath through him."

But this is not so for the wicked, as seen in John 3:36: "He that believeth on the Son hath everlasting life: and he that believeth not the Son shall not see life; but the wrath of God abideth on him."

But they that wait upon the LORD shall renew their strength; they shall mount up with wings as eagles; they shall run, and not be weary; and they shall walk, and not faint. (Isaiah 40:31)

10

CELEBRATE THE VICTORIES GIVE ALL PRAISE AND GLORY TO THE LORD!

Summary

The Christian soldier must celebrate the Lord's victory in all things.

The importance of rest and celebration

> Thine, O LORD, is the greatness, and the power, and the glory, and the victory, and the majesty: for all that is in the heaven and in the earth is thine; thine is the kingdom, O LORD, and thou art exalted as head above all. (1 Chronicles 29:11)

> O sing unto the LORD a new song; for he hath done marvellous things: his right hand, and his holy arm, hath gotten him the victory. (Psalm 98:1)

> For whatsoever is born of God overcometh
> the world: and this is the victory that overcometh
> the world, even our faith. (1 John 5:4)

> But thanks be to God, which giveth us
> the victory through our Lord Jesus Christ. (1
> Corinthians 15:57)

The Lord has lifted His sovereign scepter usward. He has rent the veil from top to bottom. He has opened Himself that we, His children, may come in.

> Oh that men would praise the LORD for
> his goodness, and for his wonderful works to the
> children of men! (Psalm 107:15)

> This is the day which the LORD hath made;
> we will rejoice and be glad in it. (Psalm 118:24)

> Rejoice in the Lord alway: and again I say,
> Rejoice. (Philippians 4:4)

Rejoice and rest in the Lord. That is the true R & R for the Christian soldier!

There is a time to rest and celebrate the fruits of your labor, knowing that the Lord has brought the increase. It is good for the soul to rest and be glad, as Psalm 68:3 says, "But let the righteous be glad; let them rejoice before God: yea, let them exceedingly rejoice." We can rejoice in the Lord's victory because we know "the end of the story!" As 2 Thessalonians 2:8 says, "And then shall that Wicked be revealed, whom the Lord shall consume with the spirit of his mouth, and shall destroy with the brightness of his coming."

Just as a soldier needs furlough, so the Christian needs rest and relaxation. This is why it is vital that a believer be part of a sound church. That is where they find renewal through the preaching of the unadulterated Word of God, true fellowship in the love of Christ, and the anointing of the Holy Spirit. We should be committed to attending the house of God, as He commands.

> Not forsaking the assembling of ourselves together, as the manner of some is; but exhorting one another: and so much the more, as ye see the day approaching. (Hebrews 10:25)

> Six days thou shalt work, but on the seventh day thou shalt rest: in earing time and in harvest thou shalt rest. (Exodus 34:21)

> *Draw nigh to God, and he will draw nigh to you.* Cleanse your hands, ye sinners; and purify your hearts, ye double minded. (James 4:8)

> Let us draw near with a true heart in full assurance of faith, having our hearts sprinkled from an evil conscience, and our bodies washed with pure water. (Hebrews 10:22)

There is great joy in drawing near and resting in the Lord, as Psalm 116 proclaims,

> Gracious is the Lord, and righteous; yea, our God is merciful. The Lord preserveth the simple: I was brought low, and he helped me. Return unto thy rest, O my soul; for the Lord hath dealt bountifully with thee. (Psalm 116:5–7)

CONCLUSION

The question we must ask ourselves is this: are we willing to step out of our comfort zone and serve the Lord? Sadly, it seems all too common that the new Christian's zeal slowly wanes into complacency. The cares of this world choke off any growth, and there is little desire for the things of God. In times of crisis, there seems to be revival, but it is short-lived. This kind of lifestyle has been possible in times of prosperity, when all is relatively well. However, that may not be true much longer. Before it is too late, we need to prepare ourselves for the tribulations to come. It is time to move from the milk to the meat of the Word of God, as we learn in 1 Corinthians 3.

> And I, brethren, could not speak unto you as unto spiritual, but as unto carnal, even as unto babes in Christ. I have fed you with milk, and not with meat: for hitherto ye were not able to bear it, neither yet now are ye able. For ye are yet carnal: for whereas there is among you envying, and strife, and divisions, are ye not carnal, and walk as men? For while one saith, I am of Paul; and another, I am of Apollos; are ye not carnal? Who then is Paul, and who is Apollos, but ministers by whom ye believed, even as the Lord gave to every man? I have planted, Apollos watered; but God gave the increase. So then neither is he that planteth any thing, neither he that watereth; but God that giveth the increase. Now he that planteth and he that watereth are one: and every man shall receive his own reward according to

his own labour. *For we are labourers together with God: ye are God's husbandry, ye are God's building.* According to the grace of God which is given unto me, as a wise masterbuilder, I have laid the foundation, and another buildeth thereon. But let every man take heed how he buildeth thereupon. For other foundation can no man lay than that is laid, which is Jesus Christ. Now if any man build upon this foundation gold, silver, precious stones, wood, hay, stubble. (1 Corinthians 3:1–12)

Every man's work shall be made manifest: for the day shall declare it, because it shall be revealed by fire; and the fire shall try every man's work of what sort it is. If any man's work abide which he hath built thereupon, he shall receive a reward. *If any man's work shall be burned, he shall suffer loss: but he himself shall be saved; yet so as by fire. Know ye not that ye are the temple of God, and that the Spirit of God dwelleth in you?* If any man defile the temple of God, him shall God destroy; for the temple of God is holy, which temple ye are. Let no man deceive himself. If any man among you seemeth to be wise in this world, let him become a fool, that he may be wise. For the wisdom of this world is foolishness with God. For it is written, He taketh the wise in their own craftiness. And again, The Lord knoweth the thoughts of the wise, that they are vain. *Therefore let no man glory in men.* For all things are yours; Whether Paul, or Apollos, or Cephas, or the world, or life, or death, or things present, or things to come; all are yours; *And ye are Christ's; and Christ is God's.* (1 Corinthians 3:13–23)

The end of time is coming. Our Lord is coming again. There will be signs and wonders as in times past. We cannot know the day or the hour, but Jesus gave us clear prophecies of the things to come. We see some of these warnings in the book of Joel.

> Gird yourselves, and lament, ye priests: howl, ye ministers of the altar: come, lie all night in sackcloth, ye ministers of my God: for the meat offering and the drink offering is withholden from the house of your God. Sanctify ye a fast, call a solemn assembly, gather the elders and all the inhabitants of the land into the house of the LORD your God, and cry unto the LORD, Alas for the day! for the day of the LORD is at hand, and as a destruction from the Almighty shall it come. (Joel 1:13–15)

> Blow ye the trumpet in Zion, and sound an alarm in my holy mountain: let all the inhabitants of the land tremble: for the day of the LORD cometh, for it is nigh at hand; A day of darkness and of gloominess, a day of clouds and of thick darkness, as the morning spread upon the mountains: a great people and a strong; there hath not been ever the like, neither shall be any more after it, even to the years of many generations. A fire devoureth before them; and behind them a flame burneth: the land is as the garden of Eden before them, and behind them a desolate wilderness; yea, and nothing shall escape them. (Joel 2:1–3)

> And the LORD shall utter his voice before his army: for his camp is very great: for he is strong that executeth his word: for the day of the LORD is great and very terrible; and who can abide it? Therefore also now, saith the LORD, turn ye even

to me with all your heart, and with fasting, and with weeping, and with mourning: And rend your heart, and not your garments, and turn unto the LORD your God: for he is gracious and merciful, slow to anger, and of great kindness, and repenteth him of the evil. (Joel 2:11–13)

And it shall come to pass afterward, that I will pour out my spirit upon all flesh; and your sons and your daughters shall prophesy, your old men shall dream dreams, your young men shall see visions: And also upon the servants and upon the handmaids in those days will I pour out my spirit. And I will shew wonders in the heavens and in the earth, blood, and fire, and pillars of smoke. The sun shall be turned into darkness, and the moon into blood, before the great and the terrible day of the LORD come. And it shall come to pass, that whosoever shall call on the name of the LORD shall be delivered: for in mount Zion and in Jerusalem shall be deliverance, as the LORD hath said, and in the remnant whom the LORD shall call. (Joel 2:28–32)

There are many prophesies of the end times in the Bible. These are just a few. Christians around the world are seeing the signs. The *globalists*, they say, are building their empire. The cryptocurrencies are threatening the US dollar, ushering in a time of fully electronically controlled financial transactions. What does that make you think of? Revelation 13:17 says, "That no man might buy or sell, save he that had the mark, or the name of the beast, or the number of his name."

Matthew 24:9 says, "Then shall they deliver you up to be afflicted, and shall kill you: and ye shall be hated of all nations for my name's sake." This is stated again in Revelation 6:11.

> And white robes were given unto every one
> of them; and it was said unto them, that they
> should rest yet for a little season, until their fel-
> low servants also and their brethren, that should
> be killed as they were, should be fulfilled.

For we know that through the power of the Holy Spirit, the brethren stand strong against the Antichrist. This will be an extremely challenging time for those witnesses who stand against Satan in the final days. As it is written,

> He had power to give life unto the image
> of the beast, that the image of the beast should
> both speak, and cause that as many as would not
> worship the image of the beast should be killed.
> (Revelation 13:15)

This is why it is so important to be strong in the Lord, to be committed and prepared to fight the good fight. This is why the Lord says, "No man that warreth entangleth himself with the affairs of this life; that he may please him who hath chosen him to be a soldier" (2 Timothy 2:4).

These are a few of the ways that we can fulfill our purpose in life for our Lord:

- *Have a zeal* for God that no man can subdue.
- *Maintain* a commitment that is unwavering—keep the right attitude.
- *Be renewed* in the mind of Christ—put off the deeds of the old man.
- *Bow* to the King of kings—be standfast and centered in Christ.

- *Seek* those things that are above through discipline and training.
- *Know* the enemy—rise after each fall and continue to fight the good fight.
- *Have faith* in God—lean not on your own understanding.
- *Put on* the whole armor of God every day.
- *Wait* on the Lord—watch and pray.
- *Rejoice* in the Lord—give all praise and glory to Him.

He hath shewed thee, O man, what is good; and what doth the LORD require of thee, but to do justly, and to love mercy, and to walk humbly with thy God? (Micah 6:8)

And now, Israel, what doth the LORD thy God require of thee, but to fear the LORD thy God, to walk in all his ways, and to love him, and to serve the LORD thy God with all thy heart and with all thy soul. (Deuteronomy 10:12)

Let us hear the conclusion of the whole matter: Fear God, and keep his commandments: for this is the whole duty of man. (Ecclesiastes 12:13)

About the Author

Sarah Elizabeth Lightell, MA, was born in Florida, where she has lived for most of her life. She started her career as an editor then became a planner for the city of Gainesville before spending nearly three decades serving with the Area Agency on Aging before retiring to pursue her dream of being a writer.

She holds an undergraduate degree in English from the University of South Florida and master of arts in urban and regional planning from the University of Florida. She resides in Central Florida with her husband, Paul, and is the mother of four adult children and grandmother of five grandchildren.